THE BIG BOOK OF
COOKIES

THE BIG BOOK OF
COOKIES

OVER 100 STEP-BY-STEP RECIPES FOR
DELICIOUS COOKIES, BISCUITS AND BARS

CATHERINE ATKINSON
WITH RECIPES BY VALERIE BARRETT
& JOANNA FARROW

southwater

This edition is published by Southwater

Southwater is an imprint of Anness Publishing Ltd, Hermes House, 88–89 Blackfriars Road, London SE1 8HA, tel. 020 7401 2077; fax 020 7633 9499, www.southwaterbooks.com; info@anness.com

© Anness Publishing Ltd 2005

UK agent: The Manning Partnership Ltd, 6 The Old Dairy, Melcombe Road, Bath BA2 3LR; tel. 01225 478444; fax 01225 478440; sales@manning-partnership.co.uk

UK distributor: Grantham Book Services Ltd, Isaac Newton Way, Alma Park Industrial Estate, Grantham, Lincs NG31 9SD; tel. 01476 541080; fax 01476 541061; orders@gbs.tbs-ltd.co.uk

North American agent/distributor: National Book Network, 4501 Forbes Boulevard, Suite 200, Lanham, MD 20706; tel. 301 459 3366; fax 301 429 5746; www.nbnbooks.com

Australian agent/distributor: Pan Macmillan Australia, Level 18, St Martins Tower, 31 Market St, Sydney, NSW 2000; tel. 1300 135 113; fax 1300 135 103; customer.service@macmillan.com.au

New Zealand agent/distributor: David Bateman Ltd, 30 Tarndale Grove, Off Bush Road, Albany, Auckland; tel. (09) 415 7664; fax (09) 415 8892

Publisher: Joanna Lorenz
Managing Editor: Judith Simons
Senior Editor: Susannah Blake
Assistant Editor: Lindsay Kaubi
Editorial Reader: Jay Thundercliffe
Production Controller: Claire Rae
Photographers: Frank Adam and Craig Robertson
Home Economists: Angela Boggiano, Silvana Franco and Jenny White
Stylist: Helen Trent
Designer: Paul Oakley
Cover Design: Balley Design Associates

Previously published as part of a larger volume, *Cookies, Biscuits, Bars and Brownies*

10 9 8 7 6 5 4 3 2 1

NOTES
Bracketed terms are intended for American readers.

For all recipes, quantities are given in both metric and imperial measures and, where appropriate, measures are also given in standard cups and spoons. Follow one set, but not a mixture, because they are not interchangeable.

Standard spoon and cup measures are level. 1 tsp = 5ml, 1 tbsp = 15ml, 1 cup = 250ml/8fl oz

Australian standard tablespoons are 20ml. Australian readers should use 3 tsp in place of 1 tbsp for measuring small quantities of gelatine, flour, salt, etc.

Medium (US large) eggs are used unless otherwise stated.

Contents

The Cookie-making Tradition

Left: *Storing home-baked cookies in a cookie jar will ensure that they stay fresh for as long as possible.*

There are differences in opinion about the origins of the word biscuit, but whether it is derived from the French *cuit* or from the Latin *biscoctus*, all agree that it means twice-cooked.

EARLY COOKIES

Originally, cookies were double-baked. They were browned for a few minutes when the oven was at its hottest, then removed and returned to finish baking when the oven was cooling down. This time-consuming process dried out the cookies so that they kept well – essential in the days before airtight containers. Not all cookies were baked; some were fried into wafers.

Rusks and ship's biscuits, which needed to keep for several months, were also baked in this way. The dough was first baked, then cooled, sliced, and dried in a gentle heat until crisp; Italian *biscotti* are still made in this manner.

During the Middle Ages, improvements were made. Sugar and spices were added to biscuits to make them more palatable and, in the late Middle Ages, it was discovered that adding beaten egg to biscuit dough made the finished cookie lighter and that ground nuts could be used instead of flour. This led to the creation of meringue, sponge and macaroon cookies.

Cookie mixtures changed significantly in the 18th and 19th centuries. The tradition of baking rusks and frying cookies virtually

No matter what age you are, there's little so enjoyable as a freshly baked cookie. They always feel like the ultimate treat, despite the fact that they're so simple to make. Cookies, in one form or another, have been around for centuries and some of the most popular cookies today derive from these original treats.

AN AMERICAN INVENTION

The term cookie was first used in the United States when early Dutch settlers brought their *koekje* (little cakes) to New York. At about the same time, wood-burning and coal-fired ovens were introduced, which made baking more reliable and the popularity of cookies and cookie-making soon spread.

Eastern European, Scandinavian and British immigrants who settled in the United States all made great contributions to the cookie-making tradition. For example, refrigerator cookies originated from German Heidesand cookies, which are made by shaping the dough into long, sausage-shaped rolls, cutting them into thin, round slices and then baking them.

In other parts of the world, the word for (and meaning of) cookie varies. In Scotland, a cookie is a sweetened bread bun that is either filled with whipped cream or thickly iced. In Britain and France, cookies are known as biscuits, while in the United States, the term biscuit is used to describe a large, soft scone.

disappeared – although in parts of Europe, India and the Middle East some cookies are still fried today – and enriched short cakes became very popular. These rich, buttery doughs still form the basis of many modern cookies.

Although savoury cheese biscuits (crackers) have their origins in medieval times, plain, savoury biscuits were not created until the 18th century. These later developed into salted crackers and cocktail savouries for nibbling with drinks.

During the 19th century, with the availability of cheap sugar and flour and chemical raising agents such as bicarbonate of soda (baking soda), cookie factories were able to open up. As the quality of factory-made cookies improved, more and more people began to buy rather than make their own cookies.

COOKIE-MAKING TODAY

In more recent years, consumers have started to turn away from foods containing artificial additives. Commercial cookies have become less popular and there has been a resurgence in home-baking.

Time-saving kitchen devices such as food mixers have helped to speed up cookie-making, and the widely available range of more unusual ingredients has opened up the possibilities for the modern cook who can make just about any cookie they want.

With the help of this book, you can learn everything you will ever need to know about cookie-making – from the basic techniques to the perfect cookie to serve with coffee, put in a lunchbox or offer as a gift.

CLASSIC COOKIES

Anzac A crunchy cookie from New Zealand, named after the Australia and New Zealand Army Corps (ANZAC). It is made with butter, golden (light corn) syrup, rolled oats and coconut.

Bath Oliver A hard, crisp savoury cracker created as a health product by Dr W. Oliver of Bath, England, in 1730.

Digestive/Graham cracker Also known as sweetmeal or wheatmeal, this moderately sweet cookie is made with brown flour. Despite its name, it has no special digestive properties.

Maria Popular in Spain, this thin, plain crisp cookie was created in England to celebrate the wedding of the Grand Duchess Maria of Austria to the Duke of Edinburgh.

Fortune Cookie During the Ming Dynasty, political resisters baked cookies containing messages detailing secret meetings and plans. The idea was revived in San Francisco in the 19th century.

Below: Modern fortune cookies contain predictions of the future.

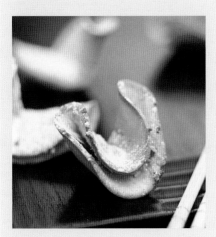

Above: Maryland cookies are one of the most popular and well-known types of chocolate chip cookie.

Jumble Well-known as early as the 17th century, this cookie was originally flavoured with rose water, aniseed or caraway seeds and tied into knots. The mixture is now made into S-shapes.

Petit Beurre This plain, crisp French cookie has been made in Nantes since the 1880s. It was created by Louis Lefevre-Utile and is also known as LU or *P'tit lu.*

Shortbread Scottish shortbread evolved from 16th-century short cakes. The main ingredients are usually flour, sugar and butter. Petticoat tails are shortbread baked in a round, named after the shape of an outspread petticoat.

Snickerdoodle A Pennsylvanian Dutch speciality, this spicy cookie contains nutmeg, nuts and raisins.

Chocolate Chip Cookies These are absolute classics; two of the best-known being Toll House cookies and chocolate chip Maryland cookies.

The Art of Making and Baking Cookies

Cookies are simple to make but there is some basic know-how that will make cookie-making even easier. This chapter explains everything you will ever need to know – from basic equipment and ingredients to making, shaping and baking different types of cookie dough; decorating and storing cookies; and making pretty cookie gifts for friends and family.

Cookie Ingredients

Most cookies are made from a few basic ingredients – butter, sugar, flour and sometimes eggs and other ingredients and flavourings. To make the best cookies, always use really fresh, good quality ingredients.

BUTTER

Unsalted (sweet) butter is best for making cookies; it has a sweet, slightly nutty taste and a firm texture, which is particularly well-suited to cookies made using the the rubbed-in method.

The temperature of butter is important. For rubbed-in cookies butter should be cold and firm but not too hard; take it out of the refrigerator 5 minutes before using. To cream butter, it should be at room temperature. This is very important if you are beating by hand. If you forget to take butter out of the refrigerator in advance, soften it in the microwave on low power for 10–15 seconds.

If you need to melt butter, dice it so that it melts more quickly and evenly. Melt the butter over a very low heat to prevent it burning

and remove it from the heat when it has almost melted; the residual heat will complete the job. If you need to brush baking tins (pans) or sheets with melted butter, use unsalted butter rather than salted, which tends to burn and stick.

STORING BUTTER

Butter should be stored in the refrigerator or freezer. It can absorb other flavours easily so protect it from strong-smelling ingredients by wrapping tightly in greaseproof (waxed) paper or foil. If possible, store in a separate compartment.

Salted butter can be stored in the refrigerator for about a month but unsalted butter should be used within 2 weeks. Alternatively, you can store unsalted butter in the freezer and transfer it to the refrigerator 1–2 days before you need it. All butter can be frozen for up to 6 months.

Left: Unsalted butter produces cookies with a wonderfully rich flavour and warm golden colour.

Above: White vegetable fat (left) and block margarine (right) work well in some cookie recipes.

OTHER FATS

Margarine This won't produce the same flavour as butter but it is usually less expensive and can be used in the same way. Block margarines are better for cookie-making, although soft margarine may be used for creaming.

White cooking fats Made from blended vegetable oils or a mixture of vegetable and animal or fish oils, white fats are flavourless and create light, short-textured cookies. They work well in highly flavoured cookies, in which you wouldn't taste the butter. Lard is an opaque white fat made from rendered pork fat and features in some traditional cookie recipes.

Oil This may sometimes be used instead of solid fat. Sunflower and safflower oils are preferable as they are light in colour with a mild taste. Olive oil has a distinctive flavour but may be added to savoury crackers.

SUGAR

There are many different types of sugar, all of which add their own distinctive character to cookies.

REFINED SUGARS

Produced from sugar cane and sugar beet, refined white sugar is 99.9 per cent pure sucrose.

Granulated sugar This has large granules and can be used in rubbed-in mixtures or to make a crunchy cookie topping.

Caster/superfine sugar This is the most frequently used sugar for cookie-making. It has a fine grain so is ideal for creaming with butter. It is also used for melted mixtures, meringue toppings and sprinkling over freshly baked cookies.

Icing/confectioners' sugar This fine, powdery sugar is used to make smooth icings and fillings and for dusting cookies. It may also be added to some piped mixtures.

Soft brown sugar This is refined white sugar that has been tossed in molasses or syrup to colour and flavour it; the darker the colour, the more intense the flavour. It makes moister cookies than white sugar, so never substitute one for the other.

UNREFINED SUGARS

Derived from raw sugar cane, these retain some molasses. They often have a more intense flavour but tend to be less sweet than refined sugars.

Golden caster/superfine sugar and granulated sugar These are pale gold and are used in the same way as their white counterparts.

Demerara/raw sugar This rich golden sugar has a slight toffee flavour. The grains are large so it is only used in cookie doughs if a crunchy texture is required. It is good for sprinkling over cookies before they are baked.

Above: (Left to right) Soft brown sugar and demerara (raw) sugar give cookies a slightly caramel taste.

Muscovado/molasses sugar

This fine-textured, moist soft brown sugar may has a treacly flavour.

STORING SUGAR

Sugar should always be stored in an airtight container. If white sugar forms clumps, break it up with your fingers. If brown sugar dries out and hardens, warm it in the microwave for about 1 minute.

OTHER SWEETENERS

There are many other ingredients that can be used as sweeteners.

Golden/light corn syrup Slightly less sweet than sugar, this produces moist, sticky cookies and is often used in no-bake recipes.

Maple syrup Thinner than golden syrup, this has a distinctive flavour.

Honey Use blended honey in cookie doughs as the flavour of milder honeys will be lost.

Malt extract This concentrated extract made from barley has a distinctive flavour, thick consistency and dark, almost black colour.

Molasses A by-product of sugar refining, molasses looks like malt extract but has a slightly bitter taste.

Above:
Coarse-grained granular sugar is good for sprinkling.

Left: Fine-grained caster sugar is widely used in cookie doughs.

FLOUR

Most cookie recipes use plain (all-purpose) flour as it has a low gluten content, resulting in a crumbly texture. The grains are processed then treated with chlorine to make the flour whiter. You can also buy unbleached flour, which has a greyish colour. Some flour is pre-sifted but you should sift it anyway as the contents tend to settle during storage. Flour, even the same type and brand, may vary slightly, so always hold a few drops of liquid back in case they aren't needed.

SELF-RAISING FLOUR

Known as self-rising flour in the United States, this flour contains raising agents that make cookies spread and rise, giving them a lighter texture. If you run out of self-raising flour, you can substitute plain flour, adding 5ml/1 tsp baking powder to each 115g/4oz/1 cup. Self-raising flour should not be kept for longer than 3 months because raising agents gradually deteriorate.

Left: *Wholemeal (whole-wheat) flour gives cookies a lovely taste.*

WHOLEMEAL FLOUR

Also known as whole-wheat flour, this is milled from the entire wheat kernel and contains all the nutrients and flavour of wheat. It is coarser than white flour, giving a heavier result. It absorbs more liquid than white flour so recipes should be adjusted if wholemeal flour is used.

Brown (wheatmeal) flour contains only 80–90 per cent of the bran and wheat germ and has a finer texture and milder taste.

NON-WHEAT FLOURS

These can be great for cookie making, although some should be combined with wheat flour.

Potato flour This fine powder is made from potato starch and can be mixed with wheat flour to give a lighter texture to cookies.

Chestnut flour This light brown, nutty flavoured flour is made from ground chestnuts and is often sold in Italian delicatessens.

Cornmeal Also known as polenta or maizemeal, this is bright yellow and coarse or medium ground.

Cornflour/cornstarch This fine white powder is made from the middle of the maize kernel. It is often used in piped cookie mixtures to give a smooth texture.

Soya flour Made from soya beans, this has a distinctive nutty flavour. It has a high protein content. Medium- and low-fat varieties are available.

Rice flour This is made by finely grinding polished white rice and is used in many cookie recipes, to give a short, slightly crumbly texture.

Above: *Rice flour is often added to shortbread to give a crumbly texture.*

Left: *Cornmeal produces cookies with a golden colour, delicious flavour and distinctive texture.*

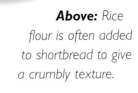

GLUTEN-FREE BAKING

Some people are allergic or intolerant to the protein gluten, which is found in both wheat and rye. Specially produced gluten-free and wheat-free flour mixtures can be used for baking, as can any of the naturally gluten-free flours such as cornmeal, potato flour, rice flour and soya flour.

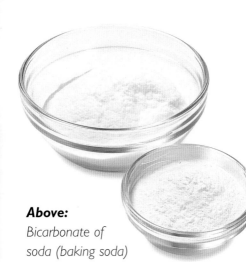

Above:
Bicarbonate of soda (baking soda) and baking powder give cookies a lighter texture.

RAISING AGENTS

Although cookies are usually made with plain (all-purpose) flour, raising agents may be added to give them a lighter texture. Raising agents make cookies spread more, so space them well apart for baking.

Raising agents react when they come in contact with water and produce carbon dioxide bubbles that make the cookie rise during baking. Cookie doughs containing raising agents must therefore be shaped and baked as soon as liquid is added. Store raising agents in a dry place and use within their use-by date because they deteriorate with age, becoming less effective.

Baking powder This is a mixture of alkaline bicarbonate of soda (baking soda) and an acid such as cream of tartar.

Bicarbonate of soda/ baking soda This can be added to a cookie mixture that contains an acidic ingredient.

Right: *Eggs are widely used in cookie-making and can help to produce rich, golden cookies with a great flavour.*

EGGS

These are used to enrich cookie doughs and bind dry ingredients. They are often included in rolled doughs because they prevent the mixture from spreading too much during baking. If a recipe does not specify the size of an egg, use a medium (US large) one.

For baking, eggs should be at room temperature; cold egg yolks may curdle and cold egg whites will produce less volume when whisked. Add eggs to a creamed mixture a little at a time, beating after each addition and adding 15ml/1 tbsp sifted flour if the mixture starts to curdle. Whisk egg whites in a very clean bowl and use straight away.

BUYING AND STORING EGGS

Always check the use-by date on eggs and never buy cracked, damaged or dirty eggs. A fresh egg will have a round, plump yolk and a thick white that clings closely to the yolk. Store eggs in the refrigerator, pointed-end down. Do not store near strong-smelling foods or possible contaminants such as raw meat; their shells are porous and can absorb odours and bacteria.

FRUIT, NUTS AND SEEDS

Dried, candied and crystallized fruit, nuts and seeds can be added to cookie doughs to add flavour, colour and texture, or to decorate.

DRIED FRUIT

The drying process intensifies the flavour and sweetness of the fruit. Adding dried fruit does not affect the moisture of the dough so you can usually subsitute one type of dried fruit for another in a recipe.

Vine fruit These include sultanas (golden raisins), raisins and currants. Buy seedless fruit, choosing a reliable brand or go for fruit in clear bags so that you can check its softness and colour. As dried fruit ages, a white coating may develop; it is still usable, but you should never buy it in this condition. It can be kept in an airtight container for up to a year, but is best used within 6 months. Some brands are lightly tossed in oil before packing to keep the fruits separate; uncoated vine fruits may stick together and should be pulled apart before adding to cookies.

Apricots These are produced in California and other parts of the American Pacific coast, Australia, South Africa, Turkey and Iran. Some are very dry and need to be soaked in a little liquid before using; others, usually labelled ready-to-eat, have a softer texture and sweeter flavour and are generally better for cookie-making. After picking and stoning (pitting), the fruits may be treated with sulphur dioxide to retain their colour and prevent mould growing.

Unsulphured apricots, which are darker in colour and very sticky, are also available; they should be stored in the refrigerator.

Apples and pears Dried in rings or as halved fruit, these have a chewy texture. They are best used finely chopped and added to drop cookie mixtures.

Tropical fruits Exotic fruits such as papaya and mango are available dried and have an intense flavour and vibrant colour. They are often sold in strips, which can be easily chopped with a sharp knife or snipped into small pieces with a pair of scissors. Dried pineapple and dried banana are also available and make a tasty addition to cookies.

Left: Dried fruit such as apricots and pears make a delicious, healthy addition to cookies.

Above: *Crystallized fruit such as glacé cherries and angelica can be used both as ingredients to flavour cookies and as decorations.*

Cranberries and sour cherries These are brightly coloured and add a wonderful sweet-and-sour flavour to cookies. They make a very good addition to festive cookies.

Candied and crystallized fruit Fresh fruits such as whole pitted cherries and apricots or pieces of kiwi and pineapple are steeped in sugar. The process retains the original bright colour of the fruit. Angelica, the bright green stem of the herb, is candied in this way. Because of their pretty colour, candied and crystallized fruit are usually used to decorate cookies rather than in the dough.

Crystallizing fruit takes a long time, making the fruit expensive. Candied citrus peel is cheaper and can be bought ready-chopped. However, make sure that chopped candied peel is still soft and moist as it can dry out quickly; it is better to buy whole pieces of candied peel and chop or slice it as required.

NUTS

These can be added to cookie mixtures or chopped and sprinkled over unbaked cookies. Always buy really fresh nuts in small quantities, then chop as necessary. Store in an airtight container, ideally in the refrigerator or freezer.

Almonds Sweet almonds are available ready-blanched, chopped, split, flaked (sliced) and ground.

Brazil nuts These wedge-shaped nuts are actually a seed. Their creamy white flesh has a sweet milky taste and a high fat content. Store carefully and use within a few months. They can be grated.

Cashew nuts These kidney-shaped nuts are always sold shelled and dried. They have a sweet flavour and almost crumbly texture.

Coconut White, dense coconut flesh is made into desiccated (dry unsweetened shredded) coconut and flakes. It is also possible to find sweetened shredded coconut, which is good for decorating cookies.

Below: Hazelnuts have a lovely nutty taste and can be used whole or chopped into small pieces.

Hazelnuts These are particularly good chopped and toasted, as this brings out their flavour.

Macadamia nuts Also known as Queensland nuts, these round, white, buttery nuts are native to Australia but are now also grown in California and South America.

Peanuts Strictly speaking, these are a legume not a nut, as they grow underground. Peanuts may be used raw or roasted, but do not use salted nuts unless specified.

Pecan nuts These are rather like elongated walnuts in appearance, but with a milder, sweeter flavour.

Pine nuts These are the fruits of the stone pine, which grows in the Mediterranean. Small and creamy coloured, they have an almost oily texture and aromatic flavour.

Pistachio nuts Bright green in colour, these are often used for decorating cookies.

Walnuts These are well flavoured with a crunchy texture. In the United States there are several types: white walnuts or butternuts, the large pale-shelled variety called English or Californian, and strong-flavoured, black-shelled walnuts.

SKINNING NUTS

To make skinning easier, either roast or blanch the nuts first.

To roast nuts, spread them out in a single layer on a baking sheet and roast at 180°C/350°F/Gas 4 for 10–12 minutes, until the skins split and the nuts are golden. Tip the nuts on to a clean dishtowel and rub gently to loosen and remove the skins.

To blanch nuts, place in a bowl, pour over boiling water and leave for 5 minutes. Drain, then slip them out of their skins.

SEEDS

These are a popular ingredient in wholesome cookies and savoury crackers. They can be added to cookie doughs to give a crunchy texture or sprinkled over the tops of cookies before they are baked to give an attractive finish. Sesame and poppy seeds work particularly well because of their small size. However, larger seeds such as sunflower seeds work well too.

Left: Sunflower and pumpkin seeds can be added to cookie doughs or sprinkled over unbaked cookies.

COOKIE FLAVOURINGS

There are many flavourings that can be added to cookies. They may add a subtle or strong taste, and some can also add texture.

CHOCOLATE

From cocoa-flavoured drop cookies to chocolate chip and chocolate-coated varieties, chocolate is the most popular cookie flavouring.

Dark/bittersweet chocolate
This has a bitter flavour and is the most popular chocolate for cookie-making. The degree of bitterness depends on the percentage of cocoa solids. Continental dark chocolate contains a minimum of 70 per cent cocoa solids so it is ideal for very sweet, sugar-laden cookies. Plain (semisweet) chocolate contains at least 50 per cent cocoa solids; the eating variety may contain as little as 25 per cent. It can be chopped and added to cookie doughs, but does not melt well.

Milk chocolate This contains milk powder and a higher percentage of sugar than plain chocolate. It is more difficult to melt.

White chocolate This contains no cocoa solids, only cocoa butter, milk solids and sugar. Some cheaper brands use flavourings and vegetable oil in place of cocoa butter. Brands that contain more cocoa butter are best for baking and melting. White chocolate may caramelize during baking due to its high sugar content.

Couverture This fine-quality plain, milk or white chocolate is used by professional cooks, and can be bought from specialist stores and by mail order. It melts beautifully and makes glossy cookie coatings.

Above: *Chocolate – in its many forms – is a popular cookie ingredient.*

Chocolate chips or dots These tiny chocolate pieces melt well and are easy to work with. The milk and white versions are more stable than bars of milk and white chocolate.

Chocolate cake covering This usually contains little real chocolate and is flavoured with cocoa powder. It melts well and is good for coating cookies, but has a poor flavour.

Unsweetened cocoa powder This bitter, dark powder can be added to cookie mixtures or dusted over the tops. (Drinking chocolate contains about 25 per cent cocoa powder and 75 per cent sugar. It is not suitable for baking.)

Complementary flavours Chocolate can be combined with many other flavourings. The most subtle is vanilla, which often goes unnoticed, yet greatly enhances the taste and aroma of chocolate. The bitterness of coffee can offset the sweetness of chocolate, and caramel works well, especially if the sugar is cooked until it is dark, as this helps to reduce some of its sweetness. Both mint and orange add a subtle tang to chocolate cookies, and are especially good for fillings, frostings and icings; nuts are a classic addition.

STORING CHOCOLATE

Chocolate should always be wrapped in foil and kept in a dry, cool place. In hot weather, chocolate can be kept in the refrigerator but it may develop a whitish bloom; this is the cocoa butter rising to the surface. The chocolate will still be safe to use and won't alter the flavour of cookies but it can affect the final texture of the cookies.

SPICES AND HERBS

Adding spices to cookies is a great way to add flavour. Warm spices such as cinnamon, ginger and nutmeg are mainly used in sweet cookies, while whole spice seeds such as cumin and fennel and ground ones such as coriander and chilli are great in crackers.

Vanilla is perhaps the spice most frequently added to sweet cookies, providing a fragrant, delicate flavour. Vanilla sugar is one of the easiest ways to add the flavouring. Pure vanilla essence (extract), which is distilled from vanilla pods (beans), is also a good way to add the flavour. Vanilla flavouring is a synthetic product and may not actually contain any real vanilla.

Fresh or dried herbs can be added to savoury cookie doughs or sprinkled on top before baking.

Above: Grated citrus rind can be added to cookie doughs to give them a lovely zesty citrus taste.

Some, such as rosemary, are highly pungent and should be used sparingly. Milder herbs such as mint are good in fillings, and mint essence (extract) can be added to doughs.

Above: Fresh mint can be added to delicately flavoured cookies and fillings to give them a fresh, aromatic flavour.

OTHER FLAVOURINGS

There are also a great many cookie flavourings that do not fit into a particular category. These include grated lemon, lime or orange rind, the juice of citrus fruits, rose water, orange flower water and almond essence (extract),

ALCOHOL

Spirits, sherry and liqueurs can be added to cookie mixtures instead of liquid such as milk. They can also be used to soak dried fruit. During baking the alcohol will evaporate, leaving a subtle flavour. They can also be used in glacé icings.

SALT

This helps to bring out the flavour in both sweet cookies and crackers, but add only the tiniest pinch, especially if using salted butter. Coarse crystals of sea salt can be used to sprinkle over savoury cookies to decorate.

Equipment

Most cookies can be made with nothing more sophisticated than weighing scales or calibrated measuring cups, a mixing bowl, fine sieve, rolling pin, wooden spoon, baking sheet and a wire rack. However, there are a few pieces of equipment that can make cookie-making even easier.

Electric gadgets can really speed up the whole cookie-making process and more specialist equipment such as cookie presses, shortbread moulds and piping bags can produce really professional-looking cookies.

BOWLS

Large bowls are good for mixing doughs, while medium and small heatproof bowls are good for melting butter or chocolate and beating eggs. Small and medium bowls are also useful if you need to measure out ingredients beforehand. Some people may argue that a copper or steel bowl is desirable for whisking egg whites to their maximum volume but, for cookie-making, this really is not necessary.

Left: An electric food mixer takes the hard work out of cookie-making and can be a real time saver.

Above: *A set of different sized, heatproof bowls for mixing, beating and melting ingredients is invaluable when making cookies.*

ELECTRICAL APPLIANCES

Food mixers and processors are great for creaming together butter and sugar and for beating in eggs. However, if these machines are used, dry ingredients should always be folded in by hand as it is very easy to over-mix cookie dough, which will spoil the final texture.

A food processor is particularly useful for chopping and grinding large quantities of nuts and some come with a mini bowl specifically made for such tasks.

A hand-held electric whisk can be used for beating eggs, whisking egg whites and beating together butter and sugar and it has the advantage that it can be used in a pan over heat. Choose one with three speeds and beaters that can be removed for easy cleaning.

MEASURING SPOONS, JUGS AND CUPS

A set of accurate measuring spoons is essential. Ordinary spoons vary in size so invest in a commercially produced set. For measuring larger volumes of dry ingredients and liquids, you will need a clearly calibrated measuring jug (cup). They are available in glass, plastic and stainless steel. Use a glass measuring jug for hot liquids; plastic may soften and stainless steel conducts heat.

Below: A set of special measuring spoons and jugs or measuring cups are essential for successful baking.

Above: Flexible palette knives and spatulas make cookie-making easier.

SIEVES

You should invest in a set of strong, fine sieves in at least two sizes; a large one for sifting dry ingredients such as flour, and a smaller one for dusting icing (confectioners') sugar or (unsweetened) cocoa powder over baked cookies. You can also buy dredgers with a very fine mesh or tiny holes in the top for dusting with icing sugar or cocoa powder but a sieve works just as well.

Below: A set of strong, fine-wire sieves will prove invaluable for cookie-making and last a lifetime.

SPATULAS

A flexible rubber or plastic spatula can be used to scrape every last morsel of cookie dough from the mixing bowl. They are also very useful for folding dry ingredients such as flour into a creamed or whisked mixture.

PALETTE KNIVES AND METAL SPATULAS

Wide and round-bladed palette knives and metal spatulas are essential for lifting cookies from baking sheets and can also be used for mixing liquid into cookie doughs and mixtures. Small ones are very useful for spreading cookie fillings and icing on to cookies.

WHISKS

A wire balloon whisk or hand-held rotary whisk are useful for whisking egg whites for cookies such as macaroons and for whipping cream to use in fillings. They are also good for removing lumps in icing.

Below: The flexible wires of a balloon whisk will incorporate air into everything from eggs to cream.

ROLLING PINS

These come in all shapes and sizes, some with handles and some without. Rolling pins are usually made of wood but they are also available in marble. Mini rolling pins are sometimes available, which are perfect for small children who want to help out in the kitchen. Hollow plastic rolling pins, designed to be filled with iced water, are also available. These have no special advantage over ordinary rolling pins, providing the cookie dough is sufficiently chilled before rolling out.

PASTRY BOARDS

These flat, smooth boards are good for rolling cookie dough out to an even thickness. They are made from many different materials including wood, toughened glass and marble, which remains cool to the touch however warm the weather.

Smooth, laminated plastic kitchen surfaces provide a good alternative to a separate pastry board but take care not to scratch the surface when using cookie cutters and sharp knives.

BAKING SHEETS

These are either entirely flat or have a lip along the length of one side; baking trays have a lip all around the edges. Baking sheets are preferable as they allow better air movement around the cookies, but be careful when removing cookies from the oven because they can slip off easily.

Always measure your oven before buying baking sheets to make sure they will fit. Large sheets will allow you to bake more cookies in each batch but there needs to be a small gap at either side and at the back of the baking sheet so that heat can circulate. Although

Below: Wooden rolling pins are efficient, inexpensive and very easy to clean.

non-stick varieties may save greasing or lining with greaseproof (waxed) paper; crisp cookies may not crisp quite so well on them and soft ones may spread out too much.

When buying baking sheets, always choose good-quality, heavy ones; they won't buckle in high temperatures, distort the shape of your cookies or develop hot-spots, which might cause burning. A good baking sheet can last you a lifetime. Avoid baking sheets that are very dark as they absorb more heat, which means cookies burn more easily. Dark baking sheets are intended for other kinds of baking such as bread-baking.

Left: Baking sheets can vary greatly in size, colour and quality.

TINS/PANS

These are available in many shapes and sizes from round, square and rectangular to petal-shaped. They are used for baking cookie doughs such as shortbread and bar and brownie mixtures. The cookies should be marked into squares, bars or wedges while warm, then cut and removed from the tin when cool. If possible, use tins with a dull finish rather than shiny aluminium ones, as they will give your cookies a crispier texture.

To bake bar cookies, use a rectangular tin measuring 28 x 18cm/ 11 x 7in or a square tin measuring 20 x 20cm/8 x 8in. (If you do not have a tin, you can use an ovenproof glass dish. However, this will not produce such good results and the oven temperature will need to be reduced slightly because glass takes longer than metal to heat up, but retains more heat when removed from the oven.

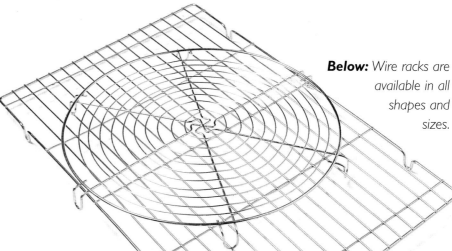

Below: Wire racks are available in all shapes and sizes.

WIRE RACKS

After baking, most cookies should be transferred to a wire rack to cool. The rack allows air to circulate, preventing trapped warmth turning into moisture and making the cookies soggy. Some cookies should be left on the baking sheet for a few minutes to firm up before transferring to a wire rack.

TIMERS

These are absolutely essential for baking. Even an extra 1 or 2 minutes in the oven can result in overbaked or burnt cookies. Many modern ovens are already fitted with a timer, but if you do not have an oven with a timer, it is well worth investing in one. The simplest timers have a rotating dial that registers any time up to 60 minutes. They are fairly accurate and are perfectly suitable for baking cookies. Modern, digital timers are very useful and accurate and will help ensure that your cookies are removed from the oven at exactly the right time. These small timers also have the advantage that you can take them with you if you need to go into another room while your cookies bake.

Above:
Cookie dough can be pressed into tins to make squares and bars.

Above: *Digital timers are inexpensive and help to ensure perfect baking.*

COOKIE CUTTERS

These come in many different shapes and sizes from the simplest plain or fluted round cutters to people-, animal-, heart- and flower-shaped ones. You will also find tiny cutters that can be used for *petits fours* and savoury cocktail snacks, and multi-sided cutters that have six different shapes arranged around a cube.

For the best results, cutters should be sharp enough to give a clear, precise outline. The top side of the cutter will usually have a smooth, rounded finish for pressing down on.

More intricate cutters will retain their shape better if they have a handle on them as this helps to keep the cutter rigid.

Below: *Metal cutters are better for cookie-making than plastic ones, which can compress the cut edges.*

Below:
Pretty shortbread moulds are usually carved from sycamore wood, which gives a sharp outline.

SHORTBREAD MOULDS

You can buy shortbread moulds that are decorated with intricate patterns. These are perfect if you are making shortbread for a special occasion or if you are making shortbread to offer as a gift. The moulds are usually made of wood. The classic shortbread mould is traditionally engraved with a Scottish thistle motif and is usually about 18cm/7in in diameter.

They are simple to use; all you need to do is press the dough into the mould with the tips of your fingers, level off the surface with a palette knife and then turn out on to a baking sheet for baking.

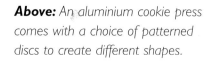

Above: *An aluminium cookie press comes with a choice of patterned discs to create different shapes.*

COOKIE PRESSES

Soft cookie dough can be shaped using a cookie press. The presses look like an icing syringe and work in a similar way. The dough is forced through a disc, which shapes the dough into a pretty cookie.

Right: Piping (pastry) bags can be filled with dough and used to make cookie shapes, or filled with icing and used to decorate baked cookies.

PIPING/PASTRY BAGS AND NOZZLES

A medium to large piping bag and a selection of both plain and fluted nozzles is useful for piping uncooked cookie dough. Smaller piping bags are extremely good for decorating baked cookies with icing or buttercream.

Originally, piping bags were made of water-proofed canvas but these tended to weep and were difficult to wash; now piping bags are made of nylon. Look for bags that are double stitched along the seams as well as glued to avoid leakage or splitting. You can also buy disposable piping bags, which are ideal for piping fine lines of melted chocolate or icing as decoration. (A small plastic bag with the corner snipped off makes a good substitute if you don't have a piping bag.)

PASTRY BRUSHES

These brushes are used for glazing unbaked cookies with milk or beaten egg, or baked cookies with a thin sugar glaze. They can also be used for brushing surplus flour from rolled cookie dough and for greasing baking sheets with oil.

The best pastry brushes have natural bristles fixed in a wooden handle, although nylon bristles are

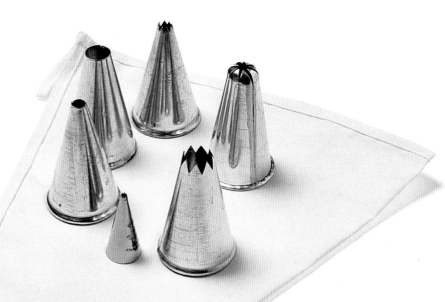

sometimes considered more hygienic. Brushes that have been used for egg glazing should be rinsed in cold water before washing in hot soapy water. Flick them dry and leave to air before using again.

Below: A pastry brush is very useful for brushing unbaked cookies with a milk or beaten egg glaze.

PASTRY WHEELS

These make quick work of cutting rolled dough into squares, rectangles or diamonds, although some skill is needed to create even-sized cookies. They are particularly good for young children who want to help with cutting out cookie shapes. They are easy to use and do not have a sharp blade. They are available from kitchenware stores and are either made from wood or stainless steel, and have a plain or fluted blade. (A pizza cutter can be used in the same way.)

Below: A fluted pastry wheel gives a pretty zigzag edge to rectangular, square and diamond-shaped cookies.

Methods of Making Cookies

There are many different ways of making cookie dough. Depending on the type of cookie you are baking, the method will vary, so it is useful to know all the techniques.

THE CREAMING METHOD

A wide variety of cookies are made using the creaming method. These include plain Shrewsbury cookies, French sablés, fork cookies, melting moments, snickerdoodles and Swiss butter cookies. The fat and sugar are creamed – or beaten – together either until just blended or, more usually, until they are well-aerated and have a light and fluffy texture. Eggs and dry ingredients are then added a little bit at a time.

The fat should be soft enough to beat easily, so remember to remove it from the refrigerator at least 30 minutes before you start mixing. Unsalted (sweet) butter is the best choice, but if you are going to use margarine, use the firm block type rather than softer margarine that is sold in tubs.

The eggs should also be at room temperature or they may curdle the creamed mixture when they are added. It is not essential to use an electric mixer or food processor for the creaming method – a wooden spoon does a perfectly good job – but it definitely makes the process easier and quicker.

Cook's Tip
Creamed mixtures have a tendency to curdle when the eggs are added. To avoid this, add the eggs a little at a time and beat well after each addition. If the mixture does curdle, beat in 15ml/1 tbsp of the flour before adding more egg.

SWISS BUTTER COOKIES
These crisp cookies are very easy to make and delicious to eat.

Makes 24
115g/4oz/½ cup unsalted (sweet) butter, softened
50g/2oz/¼ cup caster (superfine) sugar
1 egg
200g/7oz/1¾ cups plain (all-purpose) flour
30ml/2 tbsp cornflour (cornstarch)
15ml/1 tbsp ground almonds

1 Put the butter in a large mixing bowl and beat with an electric mixer or a wooden spoon until it is softened and creamy. Add the sugar and beat in until it is completely incorporated. Continue beating until the mixture is light, fluffy and much paler in colour.

2 Beat the egg lightly with a fork. Add the egg to the butter mixture, a little at a time, beating well after each addition.

3 Sift the flour and cornflour over the creamed ingredients. This will remove any lumps and incorporate air, making your cookies lighter. Add the ground almonds and stir together to make a soft dough.

4 Shape the dough into a ball, then flatten it slightly into a round – this makes it easier to roll out. Wrap the dough tightly in clear film (plastic wrap) and chill for about 30 minutes, or until the dough is fairly firm. Meanwhile, preheat the oven to 180°C/350°F/Gas 4. Lightly grease two baking sheets or line them with baking parchment.

5 Roll out the dough on a lightly floured surface to 3mm/⅛in thick. Cut the dough into rounds with a 7.5cm/3in plain cutter and place on the baking sheets. Bake for about 15 minutes until golden. Leave on the baking sheets for 5 minutes, then transfer to a wire rack to cool.

THE RUBBING-IN METHOD

Many traditional cookies, such as shortbread and digestives (Graham crackers) are made by rubbing the fat, which can be butter, margarine, white vegetable fat or lard, into the flour. The fat should be firm and cool but not straight from the refrigerator, so leave the fat at room temperature before using. Beaten eggs, milk or water may be added to bind the mixture.

CLASSIC SHORTBREAD

These buttery cookies are cooked in a round, then cut into wedges.

Makes 8 wedges

175g/6oz/1½ cups plain
  (all-purpose) flour
115g/4oz/½ cup butter, diced
  and chilled
50g/2oz/¼ cup caster (superfine) sugar,
  plus extra for sprinkling

1 Preheat the oven to 160°C/325°F/ Gas 3. Grease a baking sheet or line it with baking parchment. Sift the flour and salt into a large bowl. Use a palette knife (metal spatula) to stir in the diced butter until the pieces are coated with flour. Rub them between your fingertips, lifting the mixture and then letting it drop until it looks like fine breadcrumbs. Stir in the sugar.

2 Holding the bowl firmly, gather the dough into a ball – the warmth of your hand will help bring the dough together.

3 Gently knead the dough on a lightly floured surface for about 30 seconds until it is smooth.

4 Roll out the dough into a round about 15cm/6in in diameter and 1cm/½in thick. Transfer to the prepared baking sheet. Score the top deeply into eight sections, then prick a pattern with a fork. This will allow steam to escape during cooking and prevent the shortbread from rising in the middle. Chill the shortbread for 1 hour.

5 Sprinkle the top lightly and evenly with a little extra caster sugar. Bake the shortbread for 35 minutes, or until it is a pale, golden straw colour. Leave to cool on the baking sheet for 5 minutes, then transfer to a wire rack to cool.

MAKING RUBBED-IN COOKIES IN A FOOD PROCESSOR

This method of making cookies is especially useful where the cookie mixture contains a high proportion of fat.

1 Put the sifted flour and other dry ingredients, such as salt, into the food processor. Process for 4–5 seconds.

2 Sprinkle in the diced, chilled fat. Process for 10 seconds, or until the mixture resembles fine breadcrumbs.

3 Sprinkle any liquid, such as beaten egg, milk or water, over the mixture and, using the pulse button, process for just a few seconds until the mixture starts to hold together. Do not allow the cookie dough to form a ball in the food processor.

4 Remove the mixture from the food processor and form into a ball with your hands. Gently knead the dough on a lightly floured surface for a few seconds until smooth. Wrap the dough in clear film (plastic wrap) and then chill until fairly firm.

THE MELTED METHOD

Cookies such as flapjacks and gingernuts (gingersnaps) are made by first melting the fat and sugar or syrup together. The dry ingredients are then stirred in to make a soft dough that firms as it cools. The baked cookies become crisp as they cool, so should be quickly shaped, or left on the baking sheets for a few minutes to firm up before transferring to a wire rack.

GINGERNUTS

When baked, these spiced cookies are slightly cracked on the top.

Makes 24

50g/2oz/¼ cup butter, diced
50g/2oz/¼ cup golden (light corn) syrup
40g/1½oz/3 tbsp granulated sugar
115g/4oz/1 cup self-raising
   (self-rising) flour
5ml/1 tsp ground ginger
5ml/1 tsp bicarbonate of soda
   (baking soda)

1 Preheat the oven to 180°C/350°F/ Gas 4. Lightly grease two large baking sheets. Put the butter, syrup and sugar in a heavy pan and heat gently until just melted, stirring occasionally until the ingredients are blended. Do not let the mixture boil or some of the liquid will evaporate, altering the proportions.

2 Remove the pan from the heat and leave the mixture to cool for a few minutes. (This is particularly important if you are adding eggs, as they will cook and curdle if the mixture is too hot.) Sift the flour, ginger and bicarbonate of soda over the mixture. Stir until the mixture has blended and is smooth. The raising agents will start to work straight away, so shape the cookie dough and bake as soon as possible.

3 Place small spoonfuls of the mixture on to the prepared baking sheets, spacing the mounds of cookie dough well apart to allow room for the cookies to spread.

4 Bake the gingernuts for about 10 minutes, or until they are golden brown and the top surfaces are crazed. Leave the cookies on the baking sheets for 2 minutes to firm up, then transfer them to a wire rack to cool and crisp.

THE WHISKED METHOD

Airy cookies or crisp, delicate cookies, such as tuiles, macaroons and *langues de chat* are made by folding the dry ingredients into a whisked mixture of eggs and sugar, or into a meringue (whisked egg whites and sugar) mixture.

TUILES

These delicate cookies are named after the French curved roof tiles, which they closely resemble if they are shaped into curls while still hot.

Makes 12

1 egg white
50g/2oz/¼ cup caster (superfine) sugar
25g/1oz/2 tbsp butter, melted
   and cooled
25g/1oz/¼ cup plain
   (all-purpose) flour, sifted
flaked (sliced) almonds, for sprinkling
   (optional)

1 Preheat the oven to 190°C/375°F/ Gas 5. Lightly grease two or three baking sheets or line them with sheets of baking parchment.

2 Put the egg whites in a large, clean, grease-free mixing bowl and whisk until stiff peaks form. Gently fold in the caster sugar to make a stiff and glossy mixture. (It should resemble a meringue mixture.)

3 Trickle about a third of the melted butter down the side of the bowl and fold in with the same quantity of flour. Repeat until all the butter and flour are incorporated.

4 Place small spoonfuls of the mixture, at least 13cm/5in apart, on the prepared baking sheets, then spread out into thin rounds using the back of a spoon. Sprinkle flaked almonds over each round, if using.

5 Bake the tuiles for 6–7 minutes, or until the biscuits are pale beige in the middle and brown at the edges. Leave to cool on the baking sheets for a few seconds, then lift off carefully with a palette knife or metal spatula and cool on a wire rack. (If you want to curl the tuiles, do this while they are still hot.)

THE ALL-IN-ONE METHOD

Some cookies are made by simply placing all the ingredients in a bowl and beating them together. Drop cookies are usually made this way. This easy method can be made even faster by using a food processor, although chunky ingredients such as dried fruit and nuts may have to be stirred in after mixing the cookie dough. It is essential that the fat is soft enough to blend easily.

RAISIN COOKIES

The natural sweetness of raisins gives these cookies extra flavour and a chewy bite.

Makes 24
150g/5oz/1¼ cups plain (all-purpose) flour
2.5ml/½ tsp baking powder
pinch of salt
115g/4oz/generous ½ cup caster
  (superfine) sugar
115g/4oz/½ cup soft margarine
1 egg, lightly beaten
2.5ml/½ tsp vanilla essence (extract)
150g/5oz/1 cup seedless raisins

1 Preheat the oven to 190°C/375°F/ Gas 5. Lightly grease three baking sheets or line them with baking parchment. Sift together the flour, baking powder and salt into a mixing bowl or the bowl of a food processor. Add the sugar, margarine, egg and vanilla essence.

2 Beat with a wooden spoon or blend in a food processor until combined. Stir in the raisins.

3 Drop heaped dessertspoonfuls of the mixture about 5cm/2in apart on to the baking sheets. Bake the cookies for 15 minutes or until golden brown. Leave on the baking sheets for a few minutes then transfer to wire racks to cool.

MEASURING INGREDIENTS

Dry ingredients by weight
Whether you measure in imperial or metric, electronic and balance scales generally give more accurate readings than spring scales. Spoon or pour the dry ingredients into the bowl or tray on the scales and check the reading or dial carefully.

Dry ingredients in measuring cups or spoons
To measure a dry ingredient in a spoon, scoop it up in the spoon, then level the surface using the straight edge of a knife. If you are using measuring cups, make sure you have ¼, ⅓, ½, ⅔, ¾ and 1 cup sizes. Where a recipe calls for a scant cup, fill the cup with the dry ingredient, level with the back of a knife, then scoop out about 15ml/1 tbsp. Where a generous cup is called for, level with a knife then add about 15ml/1 tbsp.

Liquids in litres, pints or cups
Use a clear glass or plastic jug (cup) with calibrations in litres, pints or cups. Put it on a flat surface, pour in the liquid and check the markings by bending down and looking at eye level.

Liquids in spoons
Use proper measuring spoons and carefully pour in the liquid, filling it to the brim then pouring it into the mixing bowl. Do not hold the spoon over the bowl.

Drop Cookies

These are probably the simplest cookies to make. They are called drop cookies because the dough is soft enough to drop off the spoon and on to the baking sheet. The basic mixture is often made by the creaming method where butter and sugar are beaten together until light and fluffy. Eggs are then beaten in, followed by flour, raising agents and any flavourings.

CHOCOLATE CHIP COOKIES

Created in the 1930s, these were originally called Toll House cookies.

Makes 12

115g/4oz/½ cup butter, softened
115g/4oz/generous ½ cup caster (superfine) sugar
1 egg, lightly beaten
5ml/1 tsp vanilla essence (extract)
175g/6oz/1½ cups plain (all-purpose) flour
175g/6oz/1 cup plain (semisweet) chocolate chips

1 Preheat the oven to 180°C/350°F/Gas 4. Lightly grease two or three large baking sheets or line them with baking parchment. Cream the butter and sugar together in a bowl with a wooden spoon or an electric mixer until pale and fluffy. Beat in the egg and vanilla essence. Sift the flour over the butter mixture and fold in with the chocolate chips.

2 Drop tablespoonfuls of the mixture on to the prepared baking sheets. (It should fall off the spoon quite easily with a sharp jerk; if not, use another spoon to scoop it off.) Leave plenty of space between the cookies to allow for spreading.

3 Flatten each cookie slightly with the back of a fork, keeping the shape as even as possible. For dropped cookies that have a soft or cakey texture when cooked, the mixture should be left well mounded on the baking sheet and not flattened; very stiff mixtures should be more widely spread. The recipe instructions should indicate this – if you are unsure, test how much the mixture spreads by baking a single cookie.

4 Bake the cookies for about 10 minutes, or until golden. Using a palette knife or metal spatula, transfer to a wire rack to cool.

FLAVOURING DROP COOKIES

As long as you follow the basic recipe and techniques, you can make a huge variety of drop cookies. Remember, though, that some added ingredients may alter the consistency of the dough – chopped fresh fruit, for example, may make the mixture too wet, whereas rolled oats will soak up moisture, making the cookies dry and crumbly.

Chocolate Substitute 15ml/1 tbsp (unsweetened) cocoa powder for the same quantity of flour. For a chunkier texture, use coarsely chopped chocolate instead of chocolate chips. You can use milk chocolate or chocolate chips instead of the plain (semisweet) chocolate chips in the recipe on this page.

Mocha Use coffee essence (extract) instead of vanilla essence (extract).

Macadamia nut or hazelnut Add whole or coarsely chopped nuts instead of the chocolate chips. Alternatively, as nuts and chocolate are a classic combination, use 75g/3oz/½ cup of each.

Dried fruit In place of the chocolate chips, add chopped dried fruit, such as raisins, sultanas (golden raisins), apricots, glacé (candied) cherries, or a mixture of candied tropical fruit, such as pineapple, mango and papaya. Add fruit juice or milk instead of vanilla essence.

MELTED DROP COOKIES

Thin, crisp cookies, such as tuiles, florentines and brandy snaps, require the butter and sugar or syrup to be melted together first to start the caramelization process prior to baking. Such cookies usually contain little flour, which helps them spread on the baking sheet – so make sure they have plenty of room.

BRANDY SNAPS

These classic melted drop cookies have a wonderful brittle texture. They melt in the mouth to release a sweet, almost caramelized flavour.

Makes 12–14

75g/3oz/6 tbsp butter, diced
75g/3oz/scant ½ cup caster (superfine) sugar
45ml/3 tbsp golden (light corn) syrup
75g/3oz/⅔ cup plain (all-purpose) flour
5ml/1 tsp ground ginger
30ml/2 tbsp brandy
15ml/1 tbsp lemon juice

1 Preheat the oven to 190°C/375°F/Gas 5. Lightly grease several baking sheets or line them with baking parchment. Put the butter, sugar and syrup in a heavy pan. Heat gently over a low heat, stirring occasionally until the mixture has melted and becomes smooth.

2 Remove the pan from the heat. Leave the mixture to cool for a few minutes or the flour will start to cook when it is added.

3 Sift together the flour and ginger and stir into the butter mixture with the brandy and lemon juice. Leave for a further 1–2 minutes to allow the flour to absorb some of the moisture.

4 Drop teaspoonfuls of the mixture at 4cm/1½in intervals on to the baking sheets. Do not attempt to cook any more than three or four on each sheet as they will need plenty of room to spread.

5 Bake, one sheet at a time, for about 8–10 minutes, or until the cookies turn bubbly, lacy in texture and golden brown. Remove the brandy snaps from the oven and leave for about 15 seconds to firm up slightly before attempting to move them.

6 Loosen the brandy snaps from the baking sheet one at a time using a palette knife or metal spatula, and shape before cooling on a wire rack.

SHAPING UP

Some melted drop cookies need to be reshaped or neatened before, part-way through or after cooking.
Tuiles Named after the curved roof tiles in France, these may be round but are usually slightly elongated. Drop heaped teaspoonfuls of the mixture on greased or lined baking sheets then spread each into an oval, measuring 10 x 5cm/4 x 2in.
Florentines The mixture often spreads out further than the fruit and nuts. Remove from the oven 2 minutes before the end of cooking time and press back the edges into a neat shape with a palette knife to create perfect rounds, then return to the oven.
Glass cookies After baking, trim these thin, delicate cookies into shape by pressing a round metal biscuit cutter, slightly smaller than the baked cookie, into each, then pull away or break off the excess.

SHAPING MELTED DROP COOKIES

Melted drop cookies are pliable enough to be shaped into curls, rolls or baskets when they are warm. As they cool, the cookies become crisp and hard, retaining their shape.

MAKING CURLS

Tuiles are usually curled after baking. They make a pretty accompaniment to serve with desserts. Remove the cookies from the oven, lift off the baking sheet and drape over a lightly oiled rolling pin, gently curling them around. Leave them to cool and crisp before removing.

MAKING ROLLS

These tightly rolled, wand-shaped cookies are great for serving as an accompaniment to any dessert. Cigarette Russes are a classic example of a rolled cookie.

1 Shape small spoonfuls of tuile mixture into 7.5 x 5cm/3 x 2in rectangles on greased or lined baking sheets, spacing them well apart, and bake at 190°C/375°F/ Gas 5 for 6–7 minutes.

2 Carefully lift off the cookies and place upside down on a flat surface. Wind each cookie tightly around a greased wooden spoon handle.

3 Cool slightly until firm, then ease the cookies off the handles and place them on a wire rack to cool completely. Brandy snaps can be shaped in the same way, but do not turn upside-down before rolling them up.

MAKING BASKETS

You can use either large brandy snaps or tuiles to make little bowl-shaped containers for desserts such as ice cream, sorbet, fresh fruit or mousse.

1 Bake heaped tablespoonfuls of brandy snap mixture or spread heaped teaspoonfuls of tuile mixture into 12cm/4½in rounds on a large baking sheet.

2 Once cooked, leave the cookies to cool for a few seconds, then lift from the baking sheet. Mould over lightly greased, upturned ramekin dishes, pressing the edges into soft folds with your fingers.

3 If you do not have suitable ramekins, then small bowls, cups or even small oranges can be used to produce a similar effect. If you use oranges to create the basic basket shape, then remember to pat the base flat before the cookie sets so that the baskets will be stable and stand upright. Lift off once set.

Variation

To make chocolate brandy snaps, use 65g/2½oz/9 tbsp plain (all-purpose) flour and 30ml/2 tbsp (unsweetened) cocoa powder. You can always omit the ground ginger, if you prefer.

FORTUNE COOKIES

Originally forming part of an ancient Chinese tradition, these are little folded cookies made from tuile mixture. They contain short messages that predict the future and they provide lots of fun for children and adults alike.

1 Spread out teaspoonfuls of tuile mixture to 7.5cm/3in rounds on greased or lined baking sheets and bake until the edges are just turning brown.

2 Working quickly so that the cookies do not cool before they are folded, lift the cookies off the sheets with a palette knife or metal spatula. Lay a folded paper fortune message in the centre and fold the cookie in half. Bend in half again over the edge of a bowl.

3 Leave the cookies to cool and harden, then lift them off the bowl and store in an airtight container.

Rolled Cookies

A cookie dough that is rolled and cut may be a creamed, melted or rubbed-in mixture, but it must have the right consistency. If the dough is too dry it will crack and crumble; too wet and it may stick when rolling and spread during baking.

SIMPLE ALMOND COOKIES
The addition of almonds gives these cookies a delicious crunch.

Makes 24
115g/4oz/½ cup butter, softened
50g/2oz/¼ cup caster (superfine) sugar
1 egg, lightly beaten
15ml/1 tbsp ground almonds
200g/7oz/1¾ cups plain (all-purpose) flour
30ml/2 tbsp cornflour (cornstarch)

1 Preheat the oven to 180°C/350°F/Gas 4. Lightly grease two baking sheets or line them with baking parchment. Beat the butter and sugar together until creamy. Gradually add the egg, beating well after each addition, then beat in the almonds. Sift over the flour and cornflour and mix to a soft dough.

2 Lightly knead the dough on a floured surface for a few seconds, until smooth. Do not overwork the dough or the butter will start to melt and the gluten will "develop", giving the cookies a tough texture.

3 Shape the dough into a ball then flatten slightly into a round – this makes it easier when you begin to roll it out. Wrap in clear film (plastic wrap) to prevent the dough from drying out and chill for about 30 minutes, or until firm but make sure it is not too stiff to roll. If you are making a large amount of cookie dough, divide it into pieces so that you will be able to handle it more easily when rolling.

4 On a floured surface, roll out the dough lightly and evenly in one direction only to a thickness of about 3mm/⅛in. Roll from the centre to the far edge but not actually over the edge. Always roll away from you and rotate the cookie dough occasionally to prevent it from sticking and also to make sure it is evenly rolled. Avoid pulling the dough as you roll or rotate it, otherwise it may become misshapen when baked.

5 Stamp out 6.5cm/2½in rounds using a fluted cookie cutter, or use another similar-sized shape. Gather up the scraps and re-roll to make more cookies.

6 Transfer the cookies to the prepared baking sheets using a palette knife or metal spatula. Rolled out cookies shouldn't spread as much as drop cookies during baking, but you should still leave a space of at least 2.5cm/1in between each on the baking sheet. Chill the cookies for at least 30 minutes before baking them, as this helps to retain their shape.

7 Bake for 10 minutes until the cookies are a pale golden brown, making sure you rotate the baking sheets halfway through the cooking time. Remove the cookies from the oven and leave on the baking sheets for 2–3 minutes. This allows the biscuits to firm up so that they are less fragile when you handle them. Transfer the cookies to a wire rack using a metal spatula.

Cook's Tip
Cooling cookies on a wire rack allows air to circulate around them, preventing them from gathering moisture and becoming soggy as they cool.

ALL SHAPES AND SIZES

One of the greatest assets of rolled cookies is that they may be cut into any shape or size. There is a huge range of cutters available, but other ways of cutting and shaping cookies include using a pastry wheel or a knife, or even making your own template out of paper or card.

USING A KNIFE OR A PASTRY WHEEL TO SHAPE COOKIES

If you want to make squares, rectangles, triangles or bars, a sharp knife and a ruler are the perfect tools for the job. Instead of a knife, you could use a fluted pastry wheel to give an attractive edging.

1 Roll out the cookie dough to a square or rectangular shape, turning it frequently by 90 degrees. During the early stages of rolling out, push in the edges of the dough with your cupped palms to keep the shape.

2 To make square or rectangular cookies such as shortbread fingers or bourbons, use a ruler to measure the dough so that it is rolled to the appropriate shape and size, then cut with a sharp knife or pastry cutter. (For example, for custard creams, cut the dough into 4cm/1½in strips, then cut each strip at intervals of 5cm/2in to make rectangles.)

3 To make triangular cookies, cut the dough into strips then into squares, then cut each square in half diagonally to make triangles.

4 To make neat diamond-shaped cookies, cut the dough into strips and then cut diagonally across the strips to make diamonds.

MAKING A TEMPLATE

For special occasions you may want to create a more complex cookie shape for which you do not have a cutter. In this case you will need to make a template. It's probably best to avoid very intricate designs, especially those with small protrusions as these may distort or burn during baking, and will break off easily once cooked.

1 Select the design, then either draw the design straight on to a piece of thin cardboard or trace it on to tracing or greaseproof (waxed) paper first, then glue it on to cardboard. Wait for the glue to dry thoroughly before carefully cutting out the template.

2 Place the template on the rolled out cookie dough and hold it firmly in place. Using the point of a sharp knife, cut around the template to create the cookie shape.

MAKING RING COOKIES

It's hard to transfer ring cookies to baking sheets without pulling them out of shape. One solution is to place rounds of cookie dough on the baking sheet, then cut out the centres with a smaller cutter. To make perfect rings, bake round cookies, then stamp out the centres while the cookies are still warm.

1 Roll out the dough then stamp into rounds and transfer to a baking sheet. Bake the cookies according to the recipe instructions.

2 Remove the cookies from the oven and leave on the baking sheet. Using a small cookie cutter, stamp out the centres of the cookies before they have time to cool.

3 Leave the cookies on the baking sheet for 3–4 minutes, then transfer to a wire rack to cool completely.

Cook's Tips
• *To make pretty jammy sandwiches, only remove the centres from half the rounds, then sandwich the rounds and rings together with a little jam.*
• *Young children love the mini cookies that are left over after punching out holes in larger cookies. Drizzle with a little icing made from sugar and water for an extra special treat.*

MAKING MULTI-COLOURED ROLLED COOKIES

By using two or more different coloured doughs you can make a range of attractive cookies. The coloured doughs can be rolled, stamped out, then pieced together before baking, or the rolled doughs can be layered together then cut into cookie shapes.

TWO-TONE COOKIES

To make cookies with different coloured middles, leave half the dough plain and knead in a little cooled melted chocolate into the other half, or use a few drops of food colouring.

1 Roll out each piece of dough to about 3mm/⅛in thick. Stamp out an equal number of cookies (rounds or hearts) and place them on separate baking sheets. Chill for 30 minutes.

2 Using a smaller cutter, stamp out the centres from all of the cookies, then swap the plain centres for the flavoured or coloured centres and vice versa.

3 If you like, you can use a third, even smaller, cutter as well and swap the tiny centres once more to make triple-tone cookies.

PINWHEELS

These cookies are made by rolling together layers of coloured dough.

1 Divide the cookie dough into two. Leave half plain and flavour the other half by kneading in 15ml/1 tbsp sifted (unsweetened) cocoa powder and 5ml/1 tsp milk. Wrap and chill for about 30 minutes.

2 Roll out each piece of dough to a rectangle measuring 20 x 25cm/ 8 x 10in. Lightly brush the plain dough with lightly beaten egg white and place the coloured dough on top. Roll up tightly from a long side, then cut into 5mm/¼in thick slices.

NEAPOLITAN SLICES

These cookies resemble mini slices of Neapolitan ice cream.

1 Divide the dough into three. Leave one third plain, flavour one third with cocoa (as for pinwheels) and colour the remaining third pink. Wrap and chill for 30 minutes.

2 Roll out each piece of dough into a rectangle measuring 10 x 7.5cm/ 4 x 3in. Place the rectangles on top of each other, brushing between the layers with lightly beaten egg white. Cut the dough into 5mm/¼in thick slices, then cut each slice in half.

SEVEN STEPS TO SUCCESS

• Always chill the dough to firm it for at least 20 minutes and up to 1 hour before rolling. If you chill it for longer, leave it at room temperature for about 10 minutes before rolling out.
• Cookies should be rolled to a thickness of 3–5mm/⅛–¼in. Thicker cookies will have soggy centres when the outside has browned; thinner cookies will be very crisp and fragile.
• Use the minimum amount of flour when rolling out the dough. Lightly dust the work surface and the rolling pin using a flour dredger or fine sieve, sprinkling with a little more flour when needed. After cutting the cookies, brush off any excess flour with a dry pastry brush.
• If the dough is sticky, even after chilling, roll it out between two sheets of baking parchment or clear film (plastic wrap). After rolling, leave the parchment or clear film in place, slide the dough on to a baking sheet and chill before stamping out the cookies with a cookie cutter.
• When stamping out the cookies, dip the cutter into flour, then press down firmly to cut right through the dough.
• Cut cookies closely together to minimize re-rolling scraps. The first rolling is always better.
• If you haven't got a cutter, use a sharp knife or pastry wheel to cut the dough into squares or rectangles, or stamp out rounds using a thin-rimmed glass.

Piped Cookies

For this type of cookie the mixture needs to be soft enough to pipe but firm enough to keep its shape during baking. Piped cookies are usually made by the creaming method, which gives them a crumbly, airy texture and makes blending in flavourings easy. Make sure that the butter is very soft before you start as this will make mixing and piping quick and easy.

VIENNESE PIPED COOKIES

With a little practice, these cookies can be piped into any shape you like.

Makes 12
175g/6oz/¾ cup unsalted (sweet)
  butter, softened
40g/1½oz/3 tbsp icing (confectioners')
  sugar, sifted
2.5ml/½ tsp vanilla essence (extract)
175g/6oz/1½ cups plain (all-purpose) flour
40g/1½oz/3 tbsp cornflour (cornstarch)

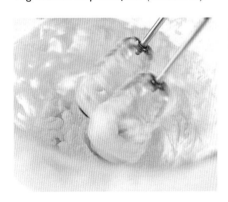

1 Preheat the oven to 180°C/350°F/ Gas 4. Grease or line two baking sheets. Cream the butter and icing sugar together until very pale and fluffy. Add the vanilla essence and beat for a few more seconds.

2 Sift the flour and cornflour together over the butter mixture and mix together until smooth.

3 Spoon the mixture into a piping (pastry) bag fitted with a large, star-shaped nozzle and pipe into the required shapes on the prepared baking sheets. Make sure the shapes are spaced well apart.

4 Bake the cookies for about 12 minutes, or until they are a pale golden colour. Leave for a few minutes on the baking sheets to firm up slightly before carefully transferring them to a wire rack with a palette knife or metal spatula to finish cooling.

Variations

Once you have mastered making and piping the basic recipe, try adding flavourings to vary the cookie mixture.
Chocolate *Substitute 30ml/2 tbsp (unsweetened) cocoa powder for the same quantity of flour.*
Coffee *Omit the vanilla essence and blend 5ml/1 tsp instant coffee powder with 5ml/1 tsp just boiled water. Leave to cool, then add to the mixture with the flour and cornflour.*
Strawberry *Use 40g/1½oz/3 tbsp strawberry flavour blancmange powder instead of the cornflour.*
Orange or lemon *Beat the finely grated rind of half an orange or lemon into the creamed mixture.*
Caramel *To give the cookies a mild caramel flavour, use unrefined icing sugar.*

PERFECT PIPING

To perfect your piping technique, follow these three simple steps.

1 Drop the nozzle into the bag, pushing it down to fit firmly. Twist the nozzle end round so that there is a twist in the bag just above it, then push the twisted section of the bag inside the nozzle to close it off.

2 Fold the top of the bag over your hand to make a "collar". Spoon in the mixture. When the bag is about half full, gently twist the top to remove the air. Holding the top of the bag, push the mixture down.

3 To pipe, hold the twisted end firmly and use the other hand to guide the nozzle. Using firm, steady pressure, pipe the shape. Push down slightly then lift up.

PIPING SHAPES

Viennese cookie mixture can be piped into all manner of shapes.

VIENNESE COOKIES

Round swirls are the classic shape for Viennese cookies.

Spoon the mixture into a piping (pastry) bag fitted with a 12mm/½in star nozzle. Pipe rosettes 5cm/2in across on to greased baking sheets, spacing them well apart.

VIENNESE WHIRLS

Sandwich two Viennese cookies together with buttercream filling and a little sieved apricot jam.

SWISS FINGERS

Pretty piped fingers are very popular, and very simple to make.

Spoon the mixture into a piping bag fitted with a 1cm/½in star nozzle. Pipe 6cm/2¼in lengths on greased baking sheets, spacing well apart.

OYSTER COOKIES

These pretty, sophisticated cookies resemble oyster shells.

Spoon the mixture into a piping bag fitted with a 1cm/½in star nozzle and pipe about five lines to make shells. Make the shape wide at one end and tapered at the other.

CHOCOLATE VANILLA SWIRLS

These two-colour cookies look lovely piped into paper cake cases.

1 Divide the Viennese cookie mixture into two equal parts and beat 15ml/1 tbsp sifted (unsweetened) cocoa powder into half of it. Spoon the vanilla mixture down one side of a piping bag fitted with a 1cm/½in star nozzle and then spoon the chocolate mixture down the other side.

2 Pipe the mixture into 12 paper cake cases in a bun tray (muffin pan) to make pretty striped swirls.

OTHER PIPED COOKIES

Many other cookie mixtures are piped to give them an even length, width and shape.

LANGUES DE CHATS

These classic French cookies are long, thin ovals with a slightly rough texture (like a cat's tongue).

Makes 18
*75g/3oz/6 tbsp unsalted (sweet)
  butter, softened*
*115g/4oz/1 cup icing (confectioners')
  sugar, sifted, plus extra for dusting*
2 large (US extra large) egg whites
30ml/2 tbsp caster (superfine) sugar
*75g/3oz/⅔ cup plain (all-purpose)
  flour, sifted*

1 Preheat the oven to 200°C/400°F/ Gas 6. Grease two baking sheets or line them with baking parchment. Cream the butter and icing sugar together until pale and fluffy.

2 In a separate bowl, whisk the egg whites to soft peaks, then add the caster sugar 15ml/1 tbsp at a time, whisking between each addition. Fold the whites into the butter mixture, then fold in the flour.

3 Spoon the mixture into a piping (pastry) bag fitted with a 1cm/½in plain nozzle and pipe 6cm/2½in lengths on to the prepared baking sheets. Allow 5cm/2in between each cookie for spreading.

4 Bake for 5–7 minutes, or until the edges are lightly browned. Leave to cool on the baking sheets for 5 minutes before transferring to a wire rack to cool completely.

FILIGREE CROWNS

These delicate, shaped cookies are made from finely piped lines of cookie mixture, which are first baked and then moulded into crowns. They make stunning little containers for desserts such as ice cream, sorbet, mousse or fresh fruit.

Makes 6

1 egg white
50g/2oz/¼ cup caster
   (superfine) sugar
25g/1oz/¼ cup plain
   (all-purpose) flour

1 Preheat the oven to 200°C/400°F/Gas 6. Draw six rectangles, each measuring about 20 x 7.5cm/8 x 3in, on six separate pieces of baking parchment.

2 Whisk the egg white and sugar together in a small mixing bowl until foamy. Sift the flour over the egg mixture and stir in thoroughly.

3 Spoon the cookie mixture into a greaseproof (waxed) paper piping (pastry) bag and snip off the tip to create a small hole. On each rectangle of baking parchment, carefully pipe thin wiggly lines from side to side to fill the marked shape, then pipe a little extra mixture down one of the long edges.

4 Bake the cookies for about 3 minutes. Remove the tray from the oven and immediately roll the cookie around a straight-sided glass.

5 Peel away the paper and stand the crowns upright. Remove the glass. If the mixture hardens before you've moulded the crowns, return to the oven for a few seconds. Cool and store in an airtight container.

SPANISH CHURROS

These little Spanish cake-cookies are made from sweetened choux pastry, which is piped into hot oil and then deep-fried. Serve sprinkled generously with cinnamon sugar.

Makes 25

75g/3oz/6 tbsp butter, diced
250ml/8fl oz/1 cup water
115g/4oz/1 cup plain
   (all-purpose) flour
50g/2oz/4 tbsp caster
   (superfine) sugar
3 eggs, lightly beaten
2.5ml/½ tsp ground cinnamon

1 Heat the butter and water in a small heavy pan until the butter has melted – do not allow the water to boil. Sift the flour and 15ml/1 tbsp of the caster sugar on to a piece of greaseproof (waxed) paper.

2 Once the butter has melted, bring to a boil, then add the flour and sugar. Remove the pan from the heat and beat the mixture vigorously. Leave to cool for 5 minutes, then gradually beat in the eggs until the mixture is smooth and glossy.

3 Half-fill a large, heavy pan or deep-fryer with oil and heat to 190°C/375°F. Spoon the mixture into a piping (pastry) bag with a 1cm/½in star nozzle. Pipe five 10cm/4in lengths of the mixture into the hot oil being careful not to cause the fat to splash or spit. Fry the churros for 2 minutes, or until golden and crisp.

4 Remove the churros from the oil with a slotted spoon and drain on kitchen paper. Repeat until all the mixture has been used. Mix the remaining caster sugar with the ground cinnamon and sprinkle over the churros. Serve warm.

Pressed Cookies

Shaped cookies are amazingly simple to make using a commercial cookie press. The press comes with a range of patterened discs and may have several settings so that a variety of shapes and sizes of cookie can be made. Choose soft-textured cookie doughs that will easily push through the press.

VANILLA FLOWERS

These pretty cookies use vanilla essence for an irresistible flavour.

Makes 25
90g/3½oz/scant ½ cup butter, softened
90g/3½oz/½ cup caster (superfine) sugar
1 egg yolk
165g/5½oz/scant 1½ cups plain
  (all-purpose) flour
5ml/1 tsp milk
5ml/1 tsp vanilla essence (extract)

1 Cream the butter and sugar together until pale and fluffy. Beat in the egg yolk. Sift the flour over the butter mixture and then fold in with the milk and vanilla essence to make a soft dough. Knead for a few seconds until smooth.

2 Fill the cookie press cylinder almost to the top with the dough and then screw on the plunger. Press out the dough on to greased baking sheets, spacing the cookies well apart.

3 Place the baking sheets in the refrigerator for at least 30 minutes, so that the cookies keep their shape while baking. Decorate with sugar or nuts, if using. Meanwhile, preheat the oven to 180°C/350°F/Gas 4.

4 Bake for 15 minutes, or until very lightly browned. Leave to cool on the baking sheets for 5 minutes, then transfer to a wire rack.

CHOCOLATE DAISIES

This dark chocolate mixture works perfectly in a cookie press.

Makes 12
175g/6oz/¾ cup unsalted (sweet)
  butter, softened
40g/1½oz/3 tbsp icing (confectioners')
  sugar, sifted
175g/6oz/1½ cups plain (all-purpose) flour
25g/1oz/2 tbsp cocoa powder
  (unsweetened)
40g/1½oz/3 tbsp cornflour (cornstarch)

1 Preheat the oven to 180°C/ 350°F/Gas 4. Grease or line two baking sheets. Cream the butter and icing sugar together until very pale and fluffy.

2 Sift the flour, cocoa powder and cornflour together over the butter mixture and thoroughly mix together until smooth.

3 Put enough of the dough into the press to fill it almost to the top, then screw on the plunger.

4 Press out the dough on to the greased baking sheets. Make sure the shapes are spaced well apart.

5 Bake the cookies for about 12 minutes until just beginning to change colour. Leave the cookies for a few minutes on the baking sheets to firm up slightly before carefully transferring them to a wire rack to cool completely.

PRESSED COOKIE TIPS AND TECHNIQUES

• To achieve a really short texture, thoroughly cream the butter and sugar until very light and fold in the flour gently.
• The dough must be very smooth to go through the fine holes in the cookie discs, so don't add chunky flavouring ingredients, such as chopped nuts, dried fruit, glacé (candied) cherries or chocolate chips.
• The dough must be sufficiently soft to be easily squeezed through the press, but firm enough to hold its shape.
• If the mixture is too firm to press, add a few drops of milk
• If the dough is slightly soft and sticks to the cookie disc, put it in the refrigerator for about 30 minutes until it has firmed.
• Pressed cookies can be decorated with ingredients such as chocolate chips, sugar crystals or nuts before baking.

Moulded Cookies

Shaping cookie dough in a mould gives a professional finish. The dough can be either shaped in a mould, then turned out for baking or baked in the shaped tin (pan) itself. It is not essential to buy special moulds, you can improvise with plain tins for both shaping and baking.

SHAPING SHORTBREAD

Shortbread moulds usually have a carved design of a thistle and are available in different sizes. The mould should be brushed with a flavourless oil the first time it is used, then wiped with kitchen paper.

1 Make one quantity of shortbread (see page 25) and roll it out to a 15cm/6in round. Press it into an 18cm/7in shortbread mould. Line a baking sheet with baking parchment.

2 Invert the mould on to the baking sheet, tapping the mould firmly to release the dough. Chill for about 30 minutes until firm.

3 Preheat the oven to 160°C/325°F/ Gas 3. Bake the shortbread for 35–40 minutes, or until pale golden. Sprinkle the top with a little caster (superfine) sugar, then leave to cool.

SHAPING MADELEINES

These French lemon cookies are baked in shell-shaped tins (pans).

Makes 15
1 egg
65g/2½oz/generous ¼ cup caster (superfine) sugar
65g/2½oz/9 tbsp self-raising (self-rising) flour
1.5ml/¼ tsp baking powder
finely grated rind of ½ lemon
65g/2½oz/5 tbsp butter, melted and cooled

1 Preheat the oven to 220°C/425°F/ Gas 7. Brush the tins with melted unsalted (sweet) butter. Chill for 10 minutes, then brush lightly with butter again, dust with flour and shake off any excess.

2 Whisk the egg and sugar until thick and pale. (The mixture should leave a trail when the whisk is lifted.) Sift over half the flour with the baking powder and fold in the lemon rind. Pour half the melted butter around the edge of the bowl and fold in gently.

3 Sift over the remaining flour, then pour in the rest of the melted butter around the edge of the bowl. Fold in gently until combined.

4 Spoon the mixture into the moulds, filling them just to the top. Bake for 10 minutes until golden. Leave for a few moments, then ease out the madeleines with a palette knife or metal spatula and transfer to a wire rack.

MAKING PETTICOAT TAILS

Shortbread is traditionally made into wedge-shaped petticoat tails.

1 Press one quantity of shortbread mixture (see page 25) into an 18cm/7in loose-based fluted flan tin (quiche pan).

2 Prick with a fork and mark into wedges using a knife. If you do not have a fluted tin, use a straight-sided sandwich tin (layer pan) and press a pattern around the edge.

MAKING SQUARES AND BARS

Cookie dough can be baked in a loose-based square or rectangular tin (pan), then cut into pieces.

1 Press one quantity of shortbread mixture into a 15cm/6in square tin or two quantities into an 18 × 28cm/7 × 11in rectangular tin.

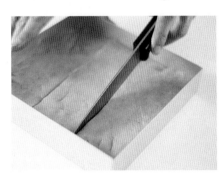

2 To cut into squares, make two cuts lengthways, then two cuts across for the square tin and four for the rectangular tin. To cut into bars, cut in half lengthways first, then cut across widthways into bars.

SMALL MOULDED COOKIES

These can be made in tiny tartlet tins (mini quiche pans) or pretty metal chocolate moulds.

Press shortbread dough into the tins or moulds until level, then bake. Alternatively, turn out the moulded rounds on to greased or lined baking sheets. Chill before baking.

SHAPING COOKIES BY HAND

You can model cookie dough into all manner of shapes. Classic hand-moulded cookies include jumbles and pretzels. Choose a dough that will retain its shape when baked.

FORK COOKIES

These are the simplest moulded cookies, made by rolling dough into balls, then flattening with a fork to make a pretty pattern on the top.

Makes 16

115g/4oz/½ cup butter, softened
50g/2oz/¼ cup caster (superfine) sugar
150g/5oz/1¼ cups self-raising
  (self-rising) flour, sifted

1 Preheat the oven to 180°C/350°F/Gas 4. Lightly grease two baking sheets. Beat the butter in a bowl until creamy, then beat in the sugar. Stir in the flour and bring the dough together with your hands.

2 Shape into walnut-size balls and place on the baking sheets, spacing well apart. Dip a fork in cold water and use to flatten the cookies.

3 Bake for 10–12 minutes, until pale brown. Leave to cool on the baking sheets for a few minutes, then transfer to a wire rack to cool.

PRETZELS

These are complicated shapes, so require a more pliable dough.

Makes 40

115g/4oz/½ cup butter, softened
115g/4oz/1 cup icing (confectioners')
  sugar, sifted
1 egg, lightly beaten
15ml/1 tbsp golden (light corn) syrup
1.5ml/¼ tsp vanilla essence (extract)
250g/9oz/2¼ cups plain
  (all-purpose) flour, sifted

1 Preheat the oven to 190°C/375°F/Gas 5. Beat the butter and sugar together until light and creamy. Beat in the egg, syrup and vanilla essence. Add the flour and stir to make a dough. Knead on a floured surface, then wrap and chill for 30 minutes.

2 Divide the dough into 40 pieces and cover the pieces that you aren't working on with clear film (plastic wrap). Roll one piece into a thin strand about 25cm/10in long.

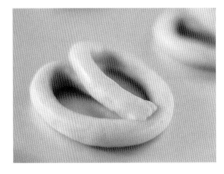

3 Create a loop with the strand, bring the ends together and press them into the top of the circle. Make the rest of the pretzels in the same way. Chill for 30 minutes.

4 Bake for 10 minutes until lightly browned, then cool on wire racks.

Bar Cookies

These are a cross between a cake and a cookie; some are thin and crunchy, others thick and chewy or light and spongy. Some bar cookies, such as brownies and flapjacks, are just a single layer, but many have two or more different layers that combine tastes and textures. Sometimes this base is partially or fully cooked first before the topping is added, then the oven temperature is lowered so that the topping doesn't overcook.

Always make bar cookies in the recommended tin (pan) size; even a small change in size will affect the cooking time and final result.

LAYERED FRUIT AND NUT BAR COOKIE

This indulgent treat combines several flavours and textures.

Makes 15

250g/9oz/2¼ cups plain (all-purpose) flour
175g/6oz/¾ cup chilled butter or
   hard margarine, diced
75g/3oz/scant ½ cup caster (superfine)
   sugar or soft light brown sugar

For the filling

115g/4oz/½ cup glacé (candied) cherries,
   coarsely chopped
50g/2oz/⅓ cup sultanas (golden raisins)
50g/2oz/½ cup almonds, chopped

For the topping

115g/4oz/½ cup butter or hard
   margarine, softened
115g/4oz/generous ½ cup caster
   (superfine) sugar
2 eggs
50g/2oz/½ cup plain (all-purpose) flour
50g/2oz/½ cup ground almonds
icing (confectioners') sugar, for dusting

1 Preheat the oven to 180°C/350°F/ Gas 4. Line the base and grease an 18 x 28 x 2.5cm/7 x 11 x 1in cake tin (pan). To make the base, sift the flour into a bowl. Additional dry flavourings such as ground spices or (unsweetened) cocoa powder (substitute for an equal quantity of flour) can be added at this stage.

2 Rub in the butter or margarine pieces until the mixture resembles breadcrumbs. Stir in the sugar. If you are adding chunky flavourings, such as coconut or chocolate chips, stir them in with the sugar. Mix with your hands until the dough comes together.

3 Press the mixture into the base of the tin. Level with the back of a spoon or a potato masher. Prick the base with a fork to let out the steam and to make sure it remains level as it cooks, then bake for 10 minutes. Remove from the oven.

4 Reduce the temperature to 160°C/325°F/Gas 3. Mix together the filling ingredients, then sprinkle evenly over the base. To make the topping, cream the butter and sugar together until pale and fluffy, then beat in the eggs. Sift over the flour and fold in with the ground almonds. Spread the topping carefully over the fruit and nuts.

5 Bake for 30 minutes, or until a light golden brown colour and firm to the touch. Check the topping is cooked by inserting a wooden cocktail stick (toothpick) into it and leaving for a few seconds; it should come out clean. Leave to cool in the tin for 15 minutes. Lightly dust with icing sugar and cut into bars.

Variations
• *Use chopped dried fruit or spread over a thick layer of jam for the filling.*
• *Try flavouring the sponge cake topping with a little finely grated citrus rind.*

TOPPING IDEAS

There are dozens of different toppings for bar cookies. The base must be fairly firm but the topping can be softer, ranging from sponge cake to caramel, and from sticky meringue to chocolate. The following ideas are sufficient for an 18 x 28cm/7 x 11in tin (pan).

CRUMBLE OR STREUSEL

This works best on top of a slightly soft or sticky base or filling such as jam, fruit purée or soft caramel.

Beat 115g/4oz/½ cup butter until creamy, then mix in 50g/2oz/¼ cup soft light brown sugar. Stir in 115g/4oz/⅔ cup semolina and 115g/4oz/1 cup plain wholemeal (wholewheat) flour until the mixture resembles breadcrumbs. Add 2.5ml/½ tsp ground ginger. Sprinkle over the base and press down. Bake at 160°C/325°F/Gas 3 for 40 minutes.

COCONUT

This light topping has a delicate flavour and lovely texture. Beat two eggs, then stir in 115g/4oz/generous ½ cup demerara (raw) sugar, 25g/1oz/3 tbsp ground rice, and 150g/5oz/1⅔ cup desiccated (dry unsweetened shredded) coconut. Spread over the base and bake at 180°C/350°F/Gas 4 for 25 minutes.

MERINGUE

This produces a wonderfully light topping that melts in the mouth,

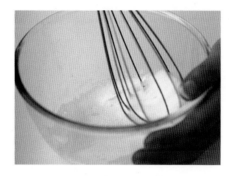

Whisk two egg whites with a pinch of salt in a clean bowl until they form soft peaks. Gradually whisk in 115g/4oz/generous ½ cup caster (superfine) sugar, a spoonful at a time, until the mixture is stiff and glossy. Fold in 2.5ml/½ tsp cornflour (cornstarch) and 5ml/1 tsp lemon juice. Spread over the base and swirl with a metal spatula to form soft peaks. Bake at 140°C/275°F/Gas 1 for 40 minutes until the meringue is set and tinged brown.

GRATED SHORTBREAD

To make this rich, buttery filling, cream together 115g/4oz/½ cup softened butter and 40g/1½oz/3 tbsp soft light brown sugar. Combine 5ml/1 tsp sunflower oil, 5ml/1 tsp vanilla essence (extract) and 1 egg yolk and beat into the butter mixture. Sift over 200g/7oz/1¾ cups plain (all-purpose) flour, 25g/1oz/¼ cup cornflour (cornstarch) and 2.5ml/½ tsp baking powder. Mix well and knead on a lightly floured surface for 30 seconds. Wrap in clear film (plastic wrap) and chill for about 30 minutes. Grate over the base or filling and press down. Bake at 150°C/300°F/Gas 2 for 45 minutes.

CITRUS CHEESECAKE

To make this zesty topping, put the finely grated rind of two lemons and two limes in a bowl with 225g/8oz/1 cup melted butter, 30ml/2 tbsp caster (superfine) sugar and three eggs. Whisk until thick and mousse-like. Sift over 40g/1½oz/⅓ cup plain (all-purpose) flour and 2.5ml/½ tsp baking powder and fold in with 30ml/2 tbsp lemon or lime juice. Pour over the base and bake at 180°C/350°F/Gas 4 for 25 minutes.

NUT CARAMEL

Put 175g/6oz/⅔ cup soft light brown sugar, 30ml/2 tbsp golden (light corn) syrup and 175g/6oz/¾ cup butter in a pan. Heat gently until the sugar has dissolved, then bring to the boil and simmer for 5 minutes, until a rich golden colour. Stir in 175g/6oz/1 cup chopped roasted unsalted peanuts. Immediately spread over base and leave to cool.

CHOCOLATE

This topping is incredibly simple and always produces great results.

Chop 350g/12oz plain (semisweet), milk or white chocolate. Sprinkle over the hot cookie base, then return to the oven for 1 minute until melted. Mark into bars when the chocolate is almost set.

BAKING THE PERFECT BROWNIE

Brownies, named after their dark rich colour, should be moist and chewy; with a sugary crust on the outside, but squidgy on the inside. There are many different recipes for brownies, varying in richness. Plainer ones rely on (unsweetened) cocoa powder alone, others on vast quantities of melted chocolate. Often, a small amount of coffee is added that is barely perceptible to the taste, but cuts through the sweetness a little. True brownies have a very high proportion of sugar and fat and most contain nuts, usually walnuts or pecan nuts.

Light versions and those made from white chocolate are often referred to as blondies. It is important to remove brownies from the oven as soon as the cooking time is up, even though they will still seem quite soft. They will firm up on standing and, if overcooked, the characteristic gooey texture will be ruined.

BROWNIE VARIATIONS

Double chocolate Add chocolate chips in place of the chopped walnuts.

Chunky choc and nut Use coarsely chopped chunks of white chocolate in place of half the walnuts.

Macadamia nut Replace the chopped walnuts with whole macadamia nuts.

Almond brownies Use almond essence and almonds instead of vanilla and walnuts.

CLASSIC CHOCOLATE BROWNIES

Richly coloured and flavoured, these are deliciously gooey and moist.

Makes 24

225g/8oz plain (semisweet) chocolate
225g/8oz/1 cup butter, diced
3 eggs
225g/8oz/generous 1 cup caster (superfine) sugar
30ml/2 tbsp strong black coffee
75g/3oz/⅔ cup self-raising (self-rising) flour
pinch of salt
150g/5oz/1¼ cups chopped walnuts
5ml/1 tsp vanilla essence (extract)

1 Preheat the oven to 180°C/375°F/ Gas 5. Grease and line a 18 x 28cm/ 7 x 11in tin (pan). Break the chocolate into squares and place in a heatproof bowl with the butter.

2 Set the bowl over a pan of barely simmering water and leave for 5–10 minutes, stirring occasionally until the mixture is melted and smooth. Remove the bowl from the pan and then leave the chocolate mixture to cool for 5 minutes.

3 In a large bowl, beat the eggs, sugar and coffee until smooth, then gradually beat in the cooled melted chocolate mixture.

4 Sift the flour and salt over the mixture, then fold in together with the walnuts and vanilla essence.

5 Spoon the mixture into the prepared tin and bake for about 35 minutes, or until just firm to the touch in the centre. (Don't bake it for any longer than this as the mixture will still be soft under the crust, but will firm up as it cools. Overcooking gives a dry result.)

6 Leave the brownies to cool in the tin then turn out on to a board, trim off the crusty edges and cut into squares. using a serrated knife and a gentle sawing action.

GREASING, LINING AND REDUCING THE SIZE OF TINS

When making bar cookies, it is important to line the baking tin (pan) with greaseproof (waxed) paper or baking parchment. This makes it much easier to lift the baked brownies or bars from the tin. If you use greaseproof paper, you will need to brush a little flavourless oil over the paper before pouring in the mixture. If you use baking parchment, the paper does not need to greased.

Base-lining Some recipes only require the base of the tin to be lined. This technique can be used to line any shape of tin, whether rectangular, square or round. Place the tin on a sheet of greaseproof (waxed) paper or baking parchment and, using a pencil, carefully draw around the tin. Using a pair of scissors, cut just inside the drawn line so that it will fit neatly inside the tin.

Using a sheet of buttered paper or a piece of kitchen paper drizzled with a flavourless oil such as sunflower or vegetable oil, grease the inside of the tin and place the lining paper in the base, pressing it into the corners.

Square and rectangular tins
To line both the base and sides of a square or rectangular tin, place the tin on a piece of greaseproof paper or baking parchment that is considerably larger than the tin. Using a pencil, draw around the tin. Cut a straight line from the edge of the paper to each corner of the square or rectangle. Turn the piece of paper over so the side marked with pencil is facing downwards. Fold in each side along its pencil line.

Grease the tin, then fit the paper inside the tin, folding the corners to fit neatly.

Round tins To line a round tin, place the tin on a piece of greaseproof paper or baking parchment and use a pencil to draw around it. Cut out the circle just inside the line. Next cut a long strip of paper about 2cm/¾in wider than the depth of the tin. (It must be long enough to wrap around the outside of the tin with 3cm/1¼in to spare.) Fold up the lower edge by 1cm/½in, then make cuts about 2.5cm/1in apart from the edge to the fold.

Grease the tin, then position the paper strip(s) around the side of the tin, so that the snipped edge sits flat on the base. Place the paper circle in the base of the tin, covering the snipped paper. Lightly grease all the paper if necessary.

Reducing tin size If the tin you are using is larger than the size required, you can reduce its size by fitting a strip of foil across the tin to make it the correct size. Make a long strip of triple thickness foil and cut it to fit three sides of the required tin.

Fold the strip of foil along one of the long edges to make a lap and fit it inside the tin to make it the required size. The weight of the mixture will hold the lap down and keep the divider in place.

Short-cut Cookies

There are occasions when you may want to make cookies in a hurry and you either don't want to turn on the oven just to bake a single batch of cookies or take the time and trouble measuring and mixing. Using ready-made cookie dough that you've either made in advance or bought, baking in a microwave oven or following a no-bake cookie recipe may provide you with the perfect solution.

REFRIGERATOR COOKIES

These are so called because the dough can be made in advance and kept in the refrigerator for up to 2 weeks before being cooked. It means that cookies can be freshly baked on demand. They are ideal for those who enjoy the pleasures of home-baked cookies, but don't always have time to make them from scratch.

The cookie dough is shaped into a log, wrapped in clear film (plastic wrap) and chilled in the refrigerator. Because the dough has a high fat content it should be chilled for at least 1 hour and preferably for longer. This will firm it to make slicing easier and will also ensure that the cookies hold their shape when cooked. The texture of the cookies is partly determined by the thickness of the slices: thinner slices will make fairly crisp cookies, thicker ones will be slightly less crisp. Some cookies such as those with chunks of chocolate or nuts are best cut in thicker slices. When baking thicker cookies, lower the temperature slightly and cook for a few minutes longer to make sure that they're cooked through.

QUICK VANILLA COOKIES

Just a few drops of vanilla essence (extract) is needed for these.

Makes 32

150g/5oz/10 tbsp butter, softened
150g/5oz/¾ cup caster (superfine) sugar
1 egg, lightly beaten
2.5ml/½ tsp vanilla essence (extract)
225g/8oz/2 cups plain (all-purpose) flour, sifted

1 Put the ingredients in a bowl and mix to a smooth dough. Lightly knead on a floured surface then roll the dough into a log shape about 5cm/2in diameter and 20cm/8in long. Wrap the log in clear film (plastic wrap) and chill for at least 1 hour or until firm enough to slice. For mini cookies, divide the dough in half and make two thinner logs.

2 Preheat the oven to 190°C/375°F/ Gas 5. Cut the dough into 5mm/¼in slices. You can dip the knife in water and wipe it dry for a clean cut.

3 When you have cut the required number of cookies, re-wrap the remaining dough and put it back in the refrigerator.

4 Place the cookies about 2.5cm/1in apart on ungreased baking sheets. Bake for 12 minutes, or until just golden around the edges. Leave on the baking sheets for 2–3 minutes, then transfer to a wire rack to cool completely. Use the remaining cookie dough within 1 week of making, or double-wrap and freeze for up to 3 months.

BOUGHT COOKIE DOUGH

If you do not have the time to make your own cookie dough, ready-made chilled or frozen dough can be bought instead. This usually comes in tubs and, although several different varieties are available, chocolate chip cookie dough is the most popular. The mixture is ready to be spooned on to greased baking sheets, then baked according to the manufacturer's instructions. Once opened, the dough can be kept in its tub in the refrigerator for several days, so that you can bake fresh batches when required.

NO-BAKE COOKIES

A range of cookies can be made by mixing melted ingredients with dry ingredients and leaving them to set. The setting agent may be chocolate, which sets firm, or syrups and marshmallows, which set to create a chewier cookie. The mixture may be spooned into paper cake cases or into a greased and base-lined shallow tin (pan), then cut into squares, bars or triangles when set.

SETTING COOKIES WITH CHOCOLATE

The simplest no-bake cookies are made with breakfast cereals such as cornflakes combined with melted plain (semisweet) chocolate, golden (light corn) or maple syrup and butter. Others may contain crushed or broken plain cookies, dried fruit and nuts rather than cereal. Always leave the melted chocolate to cool before adding the dry ingredients.

To make a basic mixture, melt 65g/2½oz/5 tbsp unsalted (sweet) butter and 175g/6oz plain chocolate together, then cool. Stir in 75g/3oz broken digestive biscuits (Graham crackers), 50g/2oz/½ cup flaked (sliced) almonds, 50g/2oz/½ cup chopped dried fruit and 50g/2oz roughly chopped white chocolate.

SETTING COOKIES WITHOUT CHOCOLATE

No-bake cookies can be set with a mixture of cooked sugar or golden (light corn) syrup combined with melted butter, marshmallows and soft toffees. The most effective mixture uses equal quantities of toffees, butter and marshmallows mixed with puffed rice cereal.

To make a basic mixture, melt 115g/4oz each of butter, marshmallows and toffees in a pan, then stir in 115g/4oz/2 cups puffed rice cereal.

MAKING ROUND COOKIES

Spoon the no-bake cookie mixture on to a sheet of greaseproof (waxed) paper or baking parchment and wrap the mixture, packing it into a fat log-shape roll about 20cm/8in long. Chill until firm, then cut into 1cm/½in slices.

MAKING COOKIE WEDGES

Some cookies are made in a round, then sliced into wedges like cakes.

1 Spoon the cookie mixture into a lightly greased and lined shallow 20cm/7in round or 15cm/6in square tin (pan). Chill for 1–2 hours, or until very firm, but not rock hard.

2 Remove the mixture from the tin, then cut into thin wedges using a sharp knife.

MAKING COOKIE TRIANGLES

Rather than making individual cookies, you can make a triangular block of cookie mixture, then slice it once it has set.

1 Line the base and three sides of a deep, greased 18cm/7in square tin (pan) with clear film (plastic wrap). Prop up one side of the tin on a box so that it is at an angle of about 45 degrees.

2 Spoon the mixture into the tin and level the surface with the back of the spoon. Leave to stand until firm, then chill until completely set. To serve, remove the block from the tin, peel off the clear film and cut into 1cm/½in triangular slices.

LAYERED NO-BAKE COOKIES

Most no-bake cookies are single-layered affairs but some are richer and have two or more layers. Bear in mind that you need to be able to slice through the cookies cleanly; so don't make one layer much more fragile than the others. Canadian nanaimo bars are a classic layered no-bake cookie. The base is made of a non-crumbly cookie and nut mixture, the filling is firm and smooth, and the chocolate topping has a little oil added to it so it doesn't crack when cut.

MICROWAVE COOKIES

Many traditional cookie recipes written with oven-baking in mind need to be adjusted for microwave cooking and there are some that simply cannot be converted successfully. Others, however, will turn out every bit as good but in a fraction of the time.

The key to cooking round cookies in a microwave is to arrange them in circles so that they cook evenly. Don't be tempted to add a cookie to the middle as it will cook more slowly than the rest.

SOFT ALMOND COOKIES

These almond cookies remain soft for some time after cooking.

Makes 12
50g/2oz/¼ cup butter, softened
50g/2oz/¼ cup soft light brown sugar
1 egg yolk
75g/3oz/⅔ cup plain (all-purpose) flour
25g/1oz/¼ cup ground almonds

1 Cream the butter and sugar together in a large mixing bowl until light and fluffy. Beat in the egg yolk. Sift over the flour and gently fold into the mixture together with the ground almonds. If you like, fold in other ingredients such as chopped glacé (candied) cherries, a mixture of dried fruit or chopped nuts.

2 Place six tablespoonfuls of the mixture in a circle on a microwave-proof dish or a piece of baking parchment cut to fit the base of the oven. Cook for 1¾–2½ minutes on high (100 per cent power) or until the surface of the cookies is dry.

3 Remove the cookies carefully from the microwave as the edges will still be soft, leave to stand for 1 minute before lifting them on to a wire rack. They will finish cooking and become firmer as they cool.

BAR MICROWAVE COOKIES

To achieve the best results with bar cookies and traybakes in a microwave, bake them in a round flan dish (quiche pan), or 4cm/1½in-deep pie plate, then cut the cookies into wedges. The centre may be difficult to cook properly in recipes such as shortbread, but this isn't a problem with high-fat, syrupy mixtures such as flapjacks.

STICKY LEMON FLAPJACKS

Made with rolled oats, flapjacks are deliciously thick and chewy.

Makes 8
75g/3oz/6 tbsp butter, diced
60ml/4 tbsp golden (light corn) syrup
115g/4oz/generous ½ cup demerara
  (raw) sugar
175g/6oz/1½ cups rolled oats
juice and finely grated rind of ½ lemon

1 Put the butter, syrup and sugar in a heatproof bowl. Microwave on medium (50 per cent) power for 3–4 minutes, stirring halfway through.

2 Stir in the oats, lemon rind and juice. Spoon the mixture into a 20cm/8in microwave flan dish and spread out.

3 Cook on full (100 per cent) power for 3–3½ minutes, or until bubbling all over. Remove from the oven and mark into wedges when warm. Leave to cool in the dish.

DIFFERENT-SHAPED COOKIES

Microwave cookies don't have to be round, but whatever the shape, they should still be arranged in a ring. Irregular-shaped cookies should be positioned with the widest part towards the outer edge of the dish. When microwaving finger or stick-shaped cookies, avoid arranging them like the spokes of a wheel; instead, place them around the edge of the dish in one or two rows.

SESAME CHEESE TWISTS

These savoury snacks are perfect to serve with soups or salads.

Makes 36

115g/4oz/1 cup plain (all-purpose) flour
1.5ml/¼ tsp salt
pinch of mustard powder
50g/2oz/¼ cup butter, diced and chilled
50g/2oz/½ cup finely grated strong-
   flavoured cheese, such as Cheddar
1 egg yolk
10ml/2 tsp cold water
30ml/2 tbsp sesame seeds

1 Sift the flour, salt and mustard powder into a bowl. Rub in the butter until the mixture resembles fine breadcrumbs, then stir in the cheese. Mix the egg yolk and water together, sprinkle over the dry ingredients and mix to a firm dough. Lightly knead on a floured surface.

2 Roll out the dough to 5mm/¼in thickness and cut into sticks about 7.5cm/3in long and 5mm/¼in wide.

3 Hold the ends of the sticks and twist them in opposite directions. Sprinkle the sesame seeds on a plate and roll the twists in them until coated. Line a microwave tray with baking parchment and arrange 12 twists in a circle on it.

4 Cook on full (100 per cent) power for 2–2½ minutes, until firm to the touch. Leave to stand for 2 minutes, then transfer to a wire rack to cool. Cook the remaining cheese twists in the same way.

Cook's Tip

There isn't a standard output or name or number for settings used by all microwave manufacturers, so cooking times are only a guide. The recipes given here are for 750-watt microwave ovens.

GETTING GOOD RESULTS

• Always use microwave-proof cookware. Glass and china are suitable, but avoid melamine, plastic and any dishes that contain metal.

• Microwaved cookies don't brown in the same way as conventionally baked ones, so coloured mixtures such as ginger and chocolate work best.

• Improve the look of microwave cookies by icing them after cooking or adding a dusting of sugar.

• Added ingredients such as chocolate, nuts and dried fruit should be cut into small, even-sized pieces.

• Don't cover the cookies during cooking to allow the steam to escape.

• Microwaved cookies continue cooking for a short time after the machine is switched off, so stop microwaving just before they are ready. Open the door during cooking to check progress. The best way to discover whether they are done is to sacrifice one and break it open; if the centre is beginning to change colour, the cookies are ready. Use the same cooking time for subsequent batches.

• Foods with a high fat or sugar content cook very quickly in a microwave and can burn easily. Always cook for the minimum time and watch carefully. Remember, if you reduce the number of cookies, the cooking time must also be reduced.

Baking Cookies

To make perfect cookies, you must take as much care with cooking them as you did with mixing and shaping the dough.

USING THE OVEN

Always allow time to preheat the oven; it will take about 15 minutes to reach the required temperature (although fan-assisted ovens may heat more quickly).

Unless the recipe instructs otherwise, bake cookies in the middle, or just above the middle, of the oven. If you are baking large quantities of cookies, do not put more than two baking sheets in the oven at once because this can cause the oven temperature to drop. This particularly applies to cookies that have been chilled beforehand.

USING BAKING SHEETS

If you are using a new baking sheet, check that it fits into the oven before you arrange the cookies on it; ideally, there should be a small gap at either side and at the back of the baking sheet to allow hot air to circulate. If you need to divide the cookies between two or more baking sheets, put the same number of cookies on each sheet, so the batches cook at the same rate. If you put two baking sheets of cookies in the oven at the same time, switch them around halfway through the cooking time. If you need to cook a second batch of cookies straight away, let the baking sheet cool before placing the next batch of raw cookies on it; a hot baking sheet might make the raw cookies spread, which will result in thin, irregular-sized cookies.

TIME AND TEMPERATURE

Baking times may vary slightly with different ovens, and can depend on how chilled the cookies were when cooking commenced. Get to know your oven. If you feel that it is either too cool or too hot, use an oven thermometer to check the temperature. If it needs adjusting, change your oven temperature dial accordingly to correct this.

Always check cookies a few minutes before the end of the suggested cooking time. Unlike cakes, they will not loose volume or sink if the oven door is opened, although you should avoid doing this too frequently or the temperature will drop and the cookies will be less crisp. Second and subsequent batches of cookies may take slightly less time to cook.

COOKING GUIDELINES

Not all cookies are the same. Different types of cookie need to be cooked in different ways and at different temperatures.

DROP COOKIES

These are baked in a moderate oven, around 180°C/350°F/Gas 4. This gives them a chance to spread out a little before they set. To make cookies that are crisp on the outside, but with a slightly soft and chewy centre, remove from the oven as soon as the edges are dark golden but the middle is still a little pale. For crisp cookies, wait until the whole cookie is lightly browned before removing from the oven. To achieve an even crisper result, spread out the mixture slightly to make a thinner layer before baking.

ROLLED, PIPED AND PRESSED COOKIES

These are usually chilled before baking to prevent them spreading too much during cooking. They are cooked in a moderate to hot oven, between 180°C/350°F/Gas 4 and 200°C/400°F/Gas 6.

1 Place the cookies on a baking sheet, then chill for 30 minutes.

2 Bake until pale golden; do not allow to colour too much.

3 Leave to cool slightly on the baking sheets, then carefully transfer to wire racks to cool completely.

REFRIGERATOR COOKIES

These cookies have a relatively high fat content and so are baked at a moderately high temperature, around 190°C/375°F/Gas 5.

1 Slice the chilled cookie mixture and arrange on ungreased baking sheets. Do not use non-stick sheets or line the sheets with baking parchment because this will make the cookies spread.

2 The cookies must be well chilled before baking, so either cook them as soon as they have been sliced or place the baking sheets in the refrigerator until ready to bake.

BAR COOKIES

This type of cookie is usually baked in a moderate to moderately low oven, between 160°C/325°F/Gas 3 and 180°C/350°F/Gas 4.

1 Bar cookies with a shortbread, pastry or crumb base are often partially baked before the topping is added. This allows the base to be cooked until crisp and firm without the topping becoming overcooked.

2 To test whether sponge or brownie mixtures are cooked, insert a cocktail stick (toothpick) into the mixture. It should come out clean.

COOLING COOKIES

Always follow the instructions in the recipe when cooling cookies. Most cookies are quite delicate so benefit from being left on the baking sheets for a minute or two to firm up, before removing to a wire rack to cool completely.

Use a thin palette knife or metal spatula to transfer cookies to wire racks. Placing them on a wire rack allows air to circulate around the them, and prevents moisture being trapped, which can make them lose their crisp texture. Don't cram too many cookies on the rack at any one time and avoid placing hot cookies on top of each other; they are likely to lose their crispness.

Cookies such as tuiles that are to be moulded into shape should be removed from the baking sheets after 30 seconds, while they are still warm and pliable. Others such as bar cookies may benefit from being allowed to cool in the baking tins (pans). Placing the whole tin on a wire rack can speed the cooling.

BAKING COOKIES AT HIGH ALTITUDE

At 3,000m/9,800ft above sea level, atmospheric pressure becomes lower, which makes liquid boil faster and causes greater evaporation. This affects cookie baking in several ways: flavours, especially sweet ones, are more concentrated; slightly more liquid is necessary; and smaller quantities of raising agents are needed. It also helps if you marginally reduce the amount of fat in recipes and increase the quantity of flour.

	ALTITUDE		
	3,000m/9,800ft	**5,000m/16,350ft**	**7,000m/22,900ft**
Sugar For each 115g/4oz/ generous ½ cup, reduce by:	10ml/2 tsp	15ml/1 tbsp	30ml/2 tbsp
Baking powder For each 5ml/1 tsp, reduce by:	0.75ml/⅛ tsp	1.5ml/¼ tsp	1.5ml/¼ tsp
Liquid For each 75ml/5 tbsp, reduce by:	5ml/1 tsp	10ml/2 tsp	30ml/1 tbsp
Oven temperature Increase by:	5°C/10°F/Gas ¼	15°C/25°F/Gas ½	20°C/35°F/Gas 1½

Cookie Decoration

Decorating cookies can add the final flourish to home-made cookies and can be one of the most enjoyable aspects of cookie-making. Cookies can be decorated before baking, while the cookies are still warm from the oven, or when they are completely cool.

DECORATING COOKIES BEFORE BAKING

Techniques for decorating unbaked cookies can range from the most simple sprinkling of sugar or nuts to brushing with a glossy glaze or painting intricate designs with edible food colouring.

SUGAR

A crunchy sugar topping is one of the easiest and most effective ways to decorate unbaked cookies. (It is also one of the most popular decorations for baked cookies.) Many different sugars can be used.

Caster (superfine) sugar can be sprinkled straight over raw cookies to give a subtle, crunchy texture. Coarse sugars such as demerara (raw) sugar and irregular-shaped coffee crystals give a crunchier result. Pretty coloured sugars and crushed white and brown sugar lumps also produce a lovely effect when sprinkled over raw cookies.

Moist cookie doughs can simply be sprinkled with sugar; drier cookies such as refrigerator or rolled cookies may benefit from being lightly brushed with a little water or milk before they are sprinkled with sugar. Alternatively, after rolling the dough, sprinkle it with sugar, then roll very lightly before cutting out the cookies.

Cookie dough that is shaped into a log before slicing can be rolled in sugar before the log is chilled and sliced. This will produce cookies with a crisp, sugary edge.

Cookies such as macaroons that produce a cracked surface during baking look particularly attractive dusted with sugar before baking. The sugar helps to accentuate the cracked effect. Flatten the balls of dough slightly, brush each with a little water and sift over a fine and even layer of icing (confectioners') sugar before baking.

NUTS

Chopped and flaked (sliced) nuts can be sprinkled over cookies in the same way as sugar. Nuts brown during baking, so avoid using on cookies that are baked at a high temperature or on cookies that are baked for a long time as the nuts may overcook.

A whole nut can be pressed into the top of each individual cookie. (This technique is best suited to soft cookie doughs.) The nuts may be decorative, or they can be used to indicate the type of cookie. For example, you might want to press a whole hazelnut into a hazelnut cookie, or an almond into an almond flavoured cookie.

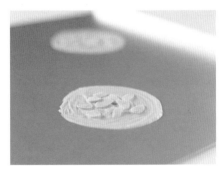

Flaked (sliced) almonds look stunning sprinkled over cookies but should be baked for no longer than 10 minutes in a moderately hot oven or they will burn. This is the classic topping for tuiles.

GLAZES

Brushing a glaze over cookies can serve two purposes, either to provide a sticky surface that nuts or sugar can stick to, or simply to give an attractive finish.

To give cookies a rich, glossy finish, use a whole beaten egg or yolk. Brush the glaze lightly and evenly on the top, without it dripping over the edges – this is especially important where raising agents have been used because it will prevent the cookies rising evenly. You can dilute the glaze by adding 15ml/1 tbsp cold water or milk and adding a pinch of caster (superfine) sugar for sweet cookies; salt for savoury ones.

Lightly beaten egg white produces a clear, shiny finish. Brush over the cookies halfway through the baking time, so that it soaks into the cookies slightly and does not set to a crackled glaze. It looks effective sprinkled with a little sugar.

PAINTED COOKIES

Edible food colouring can be painted directly on to unbaked cookies to make pretty patterns. This technique is best suited to drier, firmer cookie doughs such as rolled and refrigerator cookies.

To decorate cookies, cut the dough into shapes, place them on baking sheets and chill for 30 minutes. Beat an egg yolk and mix in a few drops of food colouring. Using a fine paintbrush, paint patterns on to the cookies, and then bake. (Remember that the yellow egg yolk may affect the colour of the food colouring.)

CANDY CENTRES

This technique is very simple to do, yet is extremely effective.

Cut out the centre of each cookie and fill it with crushed boiled sweets (hard candy). The sweets will melt during baking, then harden when cooled to make a colourful centre.

- Chopped fudge, toffee and chocolate chunks and chips add a delicious, decorative finish to drop cookies.

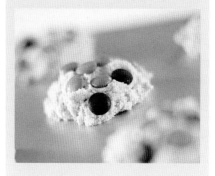

- Candy-coated chocolate buttons retain their bright colours when baked in cookies and are especially popular with young children. Mix into the dough or gently press them into the surface of the cookies.

- Halved or sliced glacé (candied) cherries and candied angelica diamonds are effective and colourful decorations.

- Pressing a pattern with the tines of a fork or marking lines on cookies with a knife look great. This also helps to prevent the cookies from rising unevenly.

SIMPLE BAKED COOKIE DECORATIONS

As with unbaked cookies, you can transform simple baked cookies into something really special with just a few simple decorating techniques. A sprinkling of sugar takes just a few seconds, while dusting a design using a stencil or writing a simple message with a food colouring pen takes only a little longer. Food colouring pens work best on refrigerator or rolled cookies that have been only lightly baked, or on firm icing.

DECORATING COOKIES WITH SUGAR

Different types of sugar can be used to give a range of effects on various baked cookies.

Icing/confectioners' sugar A light dusting of icing sugar gives plain cookies a wonderfully professional finish and is a useful way of disguising any imperfections.

Use a fine sieve or sugar dredger to give an even coating. If you want a very light layer, hold the sieve or dredger high and shake gently; for a thicker finish, keep the sieve or dredger closer to the cookies. If you are dusting pairs of cookies sandwiched together, fill them first, then sprinkle with sugar.

Caster/superfine sugar Simply sprinkling freshly baked cookies with a little caster (superfine) sugar is perhaps one of the quickest and easiest decorations to use.

Sprinkle sugar over the cookies while they are still warm so that the sugar sticks to them. (Soft light and dark brown sugars can also be used but, because they are so moist, even sprinkling is very difficult. Push through a medium sieve rather than sprinkling by hand.)

Coarse-grained sugars Granulated and demerara (raw) sugar look pretty sprinkled over cookies but, because the grains are so large, they will not stick to the cookie on their own. The easiest way to overcome this problem is to use a glaze such as beaten egg white to stick the sugar to the cookie, then return the cookies to the oven for 2–3 minutes.

Cookies such as sweet pretzels are usually coated with sugar, then grilled (broiled) until it starts to caramelize. Brush the cooled cookies lightly with egg white and sprinkle generously with demerara sugar. (Sprinkle on plenty of sugar to protect the cookie from the heat.) Place under a hot grill (broiler) for about 1 minute until the sugar is just starting to bubble. Return to wire racks to cool.

FLAVOURED SUGARS

These are a good alternative to plain caster (superfine) sugar and give cookies a subtle hint more flavour. It is possible to buy flavoured sugars, but it is just as easy to make your own.

Vanilla Put a vanilla pod (bean) in a jar of caster sugar and leave for at least 2 weeks. Refill the jar with sugar as you use it.
Sweet spice Infuse the sugar for two weeks with whole spices such as cloves. To make instant spiced sugar, use about 2.5ml/½ tsp ground cinnamon or mixed (apple pie) spice for every 30ml/2 tbsp sugar.

Citrus Add a strip of orange or lemon rind to the sugar and leave for 3 days. Shake the sugar before use as it may have become slightly damp from the rind.
Rosemary Add a sprig of fresh rosemary to the sugar and leave for 3–4 days.
Lavender Add lavender (about five heads) to the sugar and leave for 3–4 days.

DECORATING COOKIES WITH SUGAR GLAZES

Cookies such as Lebkuchen are sometimes given a slightly shiny finish with a sugar glaze. These glazes may be clear or opaque and are usually brushed over the cookies while they are still hot or warm.

LEBKUCHEN GLAZE

This semi-opaque glaze gently softens the surface of the cookie, giving it a chewy texture.

Sift 175g/6oz/1½ cups icing (confectioners') sugar into a bowl. Add 2.5ml/½ tsp almond essence (extract), 5ml/1 tsp lemon juice and 30ml/2 tbsp hot water. Mix together until smooth, then brush over the hot Lebkuchen and leave to cool.

CLEAR GLAZE

This simple sugar glaze gives cookies a lovely, glossy finish.

1 Heat 25g/1oz/2 tbsp sugar in 60ml/4 tbsp water until the sugar dissolves. Boil rapidly for 5 minutes, or until reduced by half. (The glaze can be flavoured with a strip of lemon or orange rind if you like).

2 Remove from the heat and leave to cool. Gradually beat in 115g/4oz/1 cup sifted icing sugar, then brush over warm cookies and leave to set.

STENCILLING DESIGNS

This is an easy way to decorate cookies. You can buy stencils that are specially made for cake and cookie decorating, or make your own by drawing a small design on thin cardboard and cutting it out. Make sure there is a contrast between the colour of the cookie and the dusting ingredient; icing sugar works well on chocolate cookies, while (unsweetened) cocoa powder is better on pale cookies. You can also colour icing sugar by blending cake decorator's colouring dust (petal dust) with the sugar.

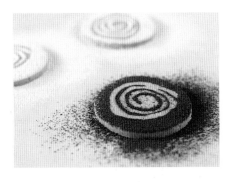

Place the stencil over the cookie. Dust with icing sugar or cocoa powder through a fine sieve, then carefully remove the cardboard.

Paper doilies can be used to make an attractive lacy pattern. Place a large doily over several cookies at once and dust liberally with icing sugar or cocoa powder.

To create a dramatic light and dark effect on cookies, lightly dust a whole cookie with icing sugar, then cover half of it with a piece of cardboard or a sheet of paper and carefully dust the other half with cocoa powder.

FOOD-COLOURING PENS

These pens look like felt-tipped pens but they are filled with edible food colouring. They come in a range of colours from primary to pastels and some are flavoured.

They can be used directly on to the cookies or on to icing. They are most effective used on rolled and cut cookies that have been baked only until light golden rather than well browned; icing must be dry and firm.

Use the decorating pens in the same way as an ordinary pen. Draw designs, write messages, or use to colour in shapes.

DECORATING COOKIES WITH ICING

Cookies can look lovely decorated with pretty coloured icing. It is important to get the consistency of icing exactly right; too thick and it will be difficult to spread; too thin and it will run off the edges and soak into the cookie.

There are many different types of icing that can be used to decorate cookies and they can range in colour from the palest pastels to vibrant primary colours. Glacé or fondant icings give a smooth, glossy finish and can be used to create simple finishing touches to the cookies, while royal icing can be swirled to give a textured pattern or piped into delicate and intricate designs. Whatever type of icing you use, iced cookies should usually be eaten within 3 or 4 days.

GLACÉ ICING

This is the simplest type of icing to make and use. It is perfect for the tops of cookies, or for drizzling and piping simple designs.

To cover 24 cookies
*115g/4oz/1 cup icing
   (confectioners') sugar
a few drops of vanilla essence
   (extract) (optional)
15ml/1 tbsp hot water
a few drops of food colouring (optional)*

Sift the icing sugar into a bowl, then add the vanilla essence, if using. Gradually stir in the hot water until the mixture is the consistency of thick cream. Add the food colouring, and continue stirring until smooth.

Top coating This is the simplest technique for coating the top of cookies with glacé icing.

Spoon a little icing on to the centre of the cookie, then carefully spread it out almost to the edges using the back of the spoon. (To make a perfect shape, pipe the outline of the shape first. Leave to dry for 1–2 minutes, then spoon in the icing and spread out to fill the shape.)

Feathered glacé icing Spoon a little icing over a cookie to cover it completely, then pipe several thin, straight parallel lines of icing in a contrasting colour across the top of the cookie.

Starting at the middle of the cookie, draw a wooden cocktail stick (toothpick) or fine skewer through the lines in the opposite direction, gently dragging the colour through the icing and creating a feathered effect on the cookie.

Cobweb icing Cover a cookie in icing, then pipe on fine, concentric circles of icing in a contrasting colour, starting from the centre and working outwards.

Draw a cocktail stick (toothpick) from the centre of the cookie to the outside edge, dividing the cookie into quarters, then repeat to divide it into eighths.

Drizzled icing Glacé icing can be drizzled or piped over cookies to give a pretty finish.

Place the cookies on a wire rack. Using a paper piping (pastry) bag or teaspoon, drizzle fine lines of icing over the cookies. You can then drizzle more icing at right angles to these first lines, if you like.

Variation
To make white glacé icing, add a few drops of lemon juice instead of vanilla essence; this enhances the whiteness.

ICING GLAZE

This is similar to glacé icing, but is flavoured with lemon juice and thinned with egg white, giving it a shinier, slightly harder set.

To cover 12 cookies

15ml/1 tbsp lightly beaten egg white
15ml/1 tbsp lemon juice
115g/4oz/1 cup icing (confectioners')
   sugar, sifted

Mix together the egg white and lemon juice in a bowl. Gradually beat in the icing sugar until the mixture is completely smooth, then place the cookies on a wire rack. Spoon the icing evenly over the cookies and leave to set.

ROYAL ICING

This icing sets hard to give a good finish so is perfect for piping designs and messages on cookies such as gingerbread. It can be coloured with a few drops of food colouring but is better left unflavoured.

To cover 30 cookies

1 egg white, at room temperature or
   7.5ml/1½ tsp albumen powder
225g/8oz/2 cups icing (confectioners')
   sugar, sifted, plus extra if necessary

1 Beat the egg white for a few seconds with a fork. (If using albumen powder, mix according to the instructions.) Mix in the icing sugar a little at a time until the mixture stands in soft peaks and is thick enough to spread. If the icing is for piping, beat in a little more icing sugar until the icing will stand in stiff peaks. Spread or pipe the icing over the cookies. Leave to set.

MAKING AND USING A PAPER ICING BAG

A paper bag for piping is easy to make once you know how.

1 Cut a piece of greaseproof (waxed) paper or baking parchment into a 25cm/10in square, then cut it in half diagonally so that you have two triangles. Hold one triangle with the longest side away from you. Curl the left-hand point over into a cone to meet the point nearest you. Curl the right-hand point over the cone.

2 Bring the points of the folded triangles together to make a neat, narrow cone. Tuck the point of paper inside the cone, fold it over and secure with sticky tape.

3 If using a nozzle, cut off the pointed end of the bag. Position the nozzle so that it fits snugly.

4 Using a palette knife or metal spatula, fill the bag with icing. Take care not to overfill the bag; half to two-thirds full is ideal.

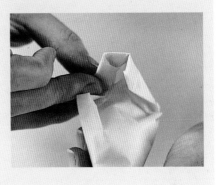

5 Fold the top corners of the bag in towards the centre, then fold over the top, firmly pushing the icing down towards the tip. Fold over the top corner again, making a pad to push with your thumb.

6 If you have not inserted a nozzle into the bag, snip a small, straight piece off the end of the bag for the icing to pass through. (It is better to snip off the small tip first. If the line of icing is too narrow, snip off a little bit more.)

7 Hold the piping bag between your middle and forefingers and push down with your thumb. Place the tip in position over the cookie, then gently push the icing through the bag using your thumb. To stop the flow of icing, release the pressure from your thumb. The icing will continue to flow for a few seconds after the pressure has stopped so you should release your thumb before you reach the end of the line.

DECORATING COOKIES WITH CHOCOLATE

The taste, texture and versatility of chocolate makes it one of the most popular ingredients for decorating cookies. It can be used to coat cookies, pipe or drizzle patterns, or even write short messages.

MELTING CHOCOLATE

For most decorating techniques, chocolate needs to be melted. Take care doing this as overheating will spoil both the texture and flavour. When melting chocolate, choose a variety with a high proportion of cocoa butter as this will melt much more easily and smoothly.

Using a double boiler Break the chocolate into pieces and put it in the top of a double boiler or in a heatproof bowl set over a pan of hot water; the water should not touch the top container. Bring the water to simmering point, then turn down the heat to keep the water at a very gentle simmer.

Check the chocolate every few minutes, turning off the heat if necessary. Stir once or twice during melting until the chocolate is completely smooth. Do not cover the bowl once the chocolate has melted or condensation will form.

Using a microwave This is a quick and simple way of melting chocolate. Bear in mind that microwaved chocolate will retain its shape, so you will need to stir the chocolate to see if it has melted.

Break the chocolate into pieces and place in a microwave-safe bowl. Melt in bursts of 30–60 seconds, checking often and reducing the time as the chocolate begins to soften. Stop microwaving before all the chocolate has melted; the residual heat in the chocolate should complete the process.

As a guide, 115g/4oz chocolate will take about 1½ minutes on full (100 per cent) power and 225g/8oz will take 2–2½ minutes. White chocolate should be melted on medium (50 per cent) power.

Using direct heat This method is only suitable for recipes where the chocolate is melted with another liquid such as milk or cream, or with other ingredients such as butter and golden (light corn) syrup.

Put the liquid ingredients in the pan, then add the chopped or broken chocolate and melt slowly over the lowest heat. When the chocolate has started to melt, turn off the heat and stir constantly until the mixture is completely smooth.

Tempering chocolate This technique is used for couverture chocolate, making it easier to work with and giving it a glossy appearance when set.

Melt the chocolate in the usual way, then pour about two-thirds of it on to a marble slab or cold surface. Using a palette knife or metal spatula, move the chocolate back and forth until it is thick and beginning to reach setting point. Return the chocolate to the bowl and melt again, stirring constantly.

USING MELTED CHOCOLATE

When you are decorating cookies with melted chocolate, handle the chocolate as little as possible and use a palette knife or metal spatula to lift and move the decorated cookies around; the warmth of your fingers will leave prints on the chocolate and make the surface dull.

Always leave chocolate-coated cookies to set at room temperature and do not store in the refrigerator unless it is exceptionally warm; chilling will cause the chocolate to lose its glossy appearance. Also make sure that the cookies are at room temperature rather than still warm from the oven or cold (if they have been stored in the refrigerator or freezer).

Coating cookies with chocolate
Before coating cookies in melted chocolate, make sure that the chocolate is just starting to cool; chocolate that is hot or even very warm will soak into the cookies and spoil the texture.

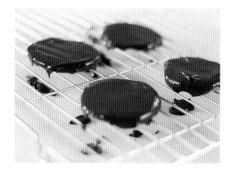

1 Place the cookies on a wire rack with a sheet of baking parchment underneath. Spoon cooled melted chocolate over each cookie, then tap the rack to help it run down the sides and to level the top. Leave to set on the rack, then cover with a second coat, if you like. Scrape the chocolate off the baking parchment, return to the bowl and re-melt to coat more cookies.

2 To decorate coated cookies, drizzle or pipe with a contrasting colour of chocolate. For a smooth surface, do this before the first layer of chocolate has set; for a raised surface, wait until the first layer of chocolate has hardened.

Dipping cookies in chocolate
Round or shaped cookies are often half-coated in chocolate and finger cookies sometimes have one or both ends dipped in chocolate. This method is simpler than completely covering cookies in chocolate. If you're planning to sandwich cookies together, they are best dipped in chocolate before filling as the warmth of the chocolate may melt the filling if dipped afterwards.

1 Melt the chocolate in a narrow deep bowl. Holding the cookie by the part that you don't want to coat, dip it briefly in the melted chocolate, then allow any excess to drip back into the bowl.

2 Place the cookie on a sheet of baking parchment and leave to set. When the chocolate is firm carefully peel off the paper. If you want to sprinkle chopped nuts or other decorations on the top, do this before the chocolate sets.

Coating florentines with chocolate
The flat underside of florentines is traditionally coated with chocolate.

Holding the florentine between finger and thumb, spread the flat base with chocolate. With the prongs of a fork, create wavy lines in the chocolate. Place the florentine on a wire rack, and leave to set

Piping chocolate
Use a small paper piping (pastry) bag with the end snipped off to pipe thin lines of chocolate.

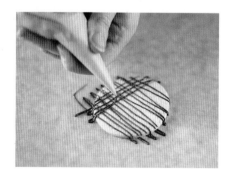

Place cookies on a sheet of baking parchment and pipe over thin lines, first in one direction, then the other.

Colouring white chocolate
You can colour melted white chocolate with cake decorator's colouring dust (petal dust). Do not use liquid or paste food colourings as these will spoil the texture of the chocolate.

Cookie Fillings

From smooth custard creams to sticky jammie sweethearts, two cookies sandwiched together are better than one. The key to a good cookie filling is to make the mixture soft enough to spread or pipe but not too moist because this can make the cookies soft and crumbly.

BUTTERCREAM

This simple cookie filling is very easy to make. Once filled, the cookies should be eaten within 3 days.

1 To make enough filling for about 12 pairs of average-size cookies, put 50g/2oz/¼ cup softened unsalted (sweet) butter in a bowl and beat with a wooden spoon until very soft, smooth and creamy.

2 Gradually stir in 90g/3½oz/scant 1 cup icing (confectioners') sugar and 5ml/1 tsp vanilla essence (extract). Beat the ingredients well with an electric mixer until they are very light and smooth.

Variations

Orange, lemon or lime buttercream
Add 15ml/1 tbsp finely grated citrus rind and replace the vanilla with juice, beating well to avoid curdling. The buttercream cannot be piped through a small nozzle because of the citrus rind.
Chocolate buttercream Blend 10ml/ 2 tsp (unsweetened) cocoa powder with 20ml/4 tsp boiling water until smooth Cool, then beat into the buttercream.
Coffee buttercream Replace the vanilla essence (extract) with 10ml/2 tsp instant coffee powder dissolved in 15ml/ 1 tbsp near-boiling water. Cool before adding to the mixture.

CRÈME AU BEURRE

This delicious buttercream has a rich taste and very smooth texture.

1 To make enough filling for about 12 pairs of average-size cookies, put 40g/1½oz/3 tbsp caster (superfine) sugar and 30ml/2 tbsp water in a small, heavy pan and heat gently until the sugar has completely dissolved. Bring to the boil and boil steadily for 2–3 minutes, until the syrup reaches 107°C/225°F on a sugar thermometer or when a little syrup pulled apart between two dry teaspoons makes a fine thread.

2 Beat 1 egg yolk in a heatproof bowl for a few seconds. Gradually pour over the syrup in a steady, narrow stream, whisking constantly. Continue whisking until the mixture is thick and cold. Beat 75g/3oz/ 6 tbsp unsalted (sweet) butter until creamy. Gradually add the egg yolk mixture to the butter, whisking well after each addition.

CHOCOLATE GANACHE

This filling is fairly soft so chill for a few minutes before using to fill cookies. It is rich, so spread thinly.

1 To make enough filling for about 20 pairs of average-size cookies. Pour 120ml/4fl oz/½ cup double (heavy) cream into a small pan and bring to the boil. Remove the pan from the heat and add 115g/4oz plain (semisweet) chocolate. Stir until melted and smooth.

2 Return the mixture to the heat and bring back to the boil. Transfer to a bowl and leave to cool. Chill for 10 minutes before using.

FILLING COOKIES WITH JAM

To make a smooth, slightly set jam filling, the jam needs to be boiled briefly to thicken it.

1 To makes enough for 16 pairs of cookies, put 120ml/8 tbsp jam in a small, heavy pan. Add 5ml/1 tsp lemon juice. Heat gently until runny, then boil for 3–4 minutes.

2 Remove the pan from the heat and leave to cool slightly, then push the jam through a fine sieve to remove any lumps. Leave the jam until barely warm, then use to sandwich the cookies together.

FILLING BRANDY SNAPS

Whipped cream, sometimes sweetened with a little sugar and flavoured with brandy or a few drops of vanilla essence (extract), makes a simple filling for these crisp rolled cookies. Using a well-chilled bowl for whipping the cream will give a lighter result.

1 To make enough cream to fill about 20 brandy snaps, pour 250ml/ 8fl oz/1 cup whipping cream into a large chilled bowl. Sift 10ml/2 tsp icing (confectioners') sugar over the cream and add about 30ml/2 tbsp brandy. Whip the mixture using an electric mixer or balloon whisk until the cream just forms soft peaks.

2 Spoon the cream into a piping (pastry) bag fitted with a large star nozzle. Push the end of the nozzle into the end of the brandy snap and squeeze gently until the brandy snap is filled to the middle. Repeat with the other end of the brandy snap.

CHOCOLATE-FILLED COOKIES

Chunks of chocolate can be baked inside the cookie to make a delicious surprise filling.

Makes about 16
150g/5oz/10 tbsp butter, softened
150g/5oz/¾ cup caster
  (superfine) sugar
1 egg yolk
15ml/1 tbsp ground almonds
225g/8oz/2 cups self-raising
  (self-rising) flour
25g/1oz/¼ cup (unsweetened)
  cocoa powder
150g/5oz plain (semisweet) chocolate
icing (confectioners') sugar, for dusting

1 Preheat the oven to190°C/375°F/ Gas 5 and grease or line two baking sheets. Cream the butter and sugar until pale and fluffy. Beat in the egg yolk and ground almonds. Sift over the flour and cocoa powder and fold into the mixture to make a firm dough. Knead for a few seconds, then wrap in clear film (plastic wrap) and chill for 30 minutes.

2 Roll out just over a third of the dough to a thickness of 3mm/⅛in and stamp out 16 rounds using a 4cm/1½in cookie cutter. Break the chocolate into squares and put one in the centre of each cookie round.

3 Roll out the remaining dough and cut into 16 larger rounds using a 5cm/2in cutter. Place these over the chocolate-covered cookie rounds and press the edges together. Bake for 10 minutes until firm. Dust the cookies with icing sugar and transfer to a wire rack. Serve warm while the filling is still soft and melted.

CLASSIC COOKIE FILLINGS

These recipes will make enough to fill 12–15 pairs of cookies.

Custard cream Melt 25g/ 1oz/2 tbsp butter in a small pan, then beat in 225g/8oz/2 cups sifted icing (confectioners') sugar, 30ml/2 tbsp milk and a few drops of vanilla essence (extract) until smooth.

Chocolate bourbon Beat together 50g/2oz/¼ cup of softened butter, 75g/3oz/¾ cup sifted icing (confectioners') sugar, 15ml/1 tbsp sifted (unsweetened) cocoa powder and 5ml/1 tsp golden (light corn) syrup until smooth.

Chocolate and orange Bring 120ml/4fl oz/½ cup whipping cream to the boil. Remove from the heat and stir in 200g/7oz chopped white chocolate until smooth. Stir in 5ml/1 tsp orange essence (extract) or liqueur.

Fudgy mocha Dissolve 10ml/ 2 tsp instant coffee powder in 5ml/1 tsp water in a heatproof bowl set over a pan of boiling water. Add four chopped chocolate-coated fudge fingers. Stir until melted, remove from the heat and whisk in 30ml/ 2 tbsp double (heavy) cream. Chill until firm enough to spread.

Honey and ginger Beat together 75g/3oz/6 tbsp softened butter, 75g/3oz/¾ cup set honey and 75g/3oz/¾ cup icing (confectioners') sugar until light and creamy. Beat in 40g/1½oz finely chopped, preserved stem ginger.

Storing Cookies

With few exceptions, cookies are best eaten on the day that they are made. Some such as American-style soft cookies are delicious when still slightly warm from the oven, but most cookies need to be cooled first to allow them to crisp. If you're not planning to eat them straight away, store them as soon as they have cooled. This will prevent crisp cookies from becoming soft and soft ones from drying out and hardening. Store crisp and soft cookies separately; if kept together, not only will their texture suffer, but the flavours may mingle as well.

SOFT COOKIES

It is essential to keep these cookies in an airtight container and, if possible, they should also be stored in the refrigerator to retain the freshly baked flavour.

Carefully pack cookies into an airtight container and seal. If the lid of the container isn't tight-fitting, put the cookies inside a plastic bag first, or cover the whole container with clear film (plastic wrap) before closing the lid. To restore the texture of soft cookies that have hardened – this may happen very quickly in dry climates – add a slice of brown bread to the container. Replace the bread daily.

CRISP COOKIES

The container for this type of cookie does not need to be absolutely airtight; unless the atmosphere is very humid, a slight flow of air will help them stay crisp.

Glass jars and ceramic containers with cork stoppers are ideal for storing crisp cookies. Place a little crumpled tissue paper in the base of the jar to help absorb any moisture. If cookies become soft, place them on a baking sheet and put in a preheated oven at 150°C/300°F/Gas 2 for about 3 minutes to re-crisp. Remove and cool on a wire rack before storing.

COOKIES IN THE FREEZER

Undecorated baked cookies can be frozen successfully. Freeze the cookies on trays, then pack into an airtight container interleaving with greaseproof (waxed) paper or baking parchment. (Avoid freezing cream-filled cookies such as brandy snaps as these will quickly become soggy.) To thaw, leave at room temperature for about 20 minutes.

Iced cookies can also be frozen in the same way, but they should be removed from the airtight container and thawed on a wire rack – the icing may be spoiled if they are left to thaw while still packed in layers.

CHILLING AND FREEZING COOKIE DOUGH

As long as cookie dough doesn't contain leavening ingredients, it can be stored in the refrigerator overnight or, in some cases, for up to a week. Cookie dough can also be frozen for up to 3 months but the flavours tend to lose their intensity after a month so, for optimum results, the dough is best frozen for just a few weeks.

To store cookie dough in the refrigerator, wrap it in clear film (plastic wrap) or place it in a bowl and cover it tightly with clear film. To freeze, wrap the dough in a double wrapping of clear film, then store in an airtight container.

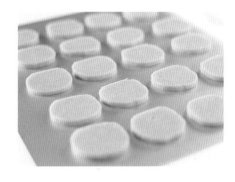

To freeze unbaked cookies, open-freeze them on trays, then pack into airtight containers, interleaving the layers with greaseproof (waxed) paper or baking parchment. Thaw unbaked cookies on baking sheets.

WHAT WENT WRONG AND WHY

Occasionally cookies don't turn out quite as you had hoped. If you have a problem when baking, try to work out why so that you can either remedy it at the time, or at least avoid it next time you bake cookies.

Problem	Cause	Remedy
The dough is very soft and won't hold its shape.	Too much liquid or fat or too little flour, or the dough has become too warm.	Always measure ingredients carefully. Chill the dough for 30 minutes before baking. If it is still too soft, work in a little extra flour.
The dough is dry and crumbly and won't hold together.	Not enough liquid or fat or too much flour, or the dough may not have been kneaded sufficiently.	Try gently kneading the dough; the warmth of your hands may bring it together. If the dough includes egg, check the right size was used. Knead in a little beaten egg, milk or soft butter.
The cookies are not evenly cooked.	The cookies are either of uneven sizes on the baking sheet; or some cookies were placed too near the edge of the sheet.	Make sure that all the cookies on a baking sheet are an even size. Leave at least a 2.5cm/1in gap around the edge of the baking sheet and turn the sheets around halfway through baking.
The cookies stick to the baking sheet.	The baking sheet was not greased or greased unevenly. Alternatively, it may have been greased with salted butter.	Use melted, unsalted (sweet) butter or oil for greasing or line the sheet with baking parchment.
The cookies crumble when removed from baking sheet.	Cookies that have a very high butter content are often more fragile than less rich ones.	Leave fragile cookies to cool on the baking sheet for at least 3 minutes before transferring to a wire rack.
The cookies are dry and too crisp on top.	The oven was too hot or the cookies were baked for too long.	If you have concerns about the temperature of your oven, use an oven thermometer. Check cookies a few minutes before end of cooking time.
The cookies spread out too much on the baking sheet.	The cookies were not chilled before baking, or, the baking sheet was over-greased when the cookies were added.	Most cookies benefit from chilling before baking. Grease baking sheets only lightly. Some cookies such as refrigerator cookies should be baked on ungreased baking sheets. Always use cold baking sheets.
The cookies are burnt on the base but not on the top.	There are a number of possible causes: baking too low down in the oven, or at too low a temperature; the baking sheets may be poor quality, or you may have used salted butter for greasing.	Check the oven temperature and bake cookies on the middle shelf. Avoid thin or very dark baking sheets. Butter burns at a lower temperature, so use oil for cookies baked at high temperatures or for a long time.

Presentation and Packaging

Whether you're making cookies to serve to guests, give as a gift or sell at a fundraising event, it is worth spending a little time on pretty presentation and attractive and elegant packaging.

All cookies should be properly stored as soon as they have cooled or, if iced or decorated, as soon as they have set and hardened. Leave gift wrapping and packaging until the last minute so that the cookies are as fresh as possible. It is often useful to include information about the cookies as well, including a list of ingredients and advice on storing.

GIFT BOXES

You can buy a huge range of pretty storage containers that make perfect packaging for cookies. Stationers and department stores sell a range of beautiful gift boxes and containers in all shapes and sizes, patterns and colours. These are the simplest way to package cookies and look stunning tied with curled ribbon or raffia.

Line the box with either crumpled tissue paper or several layers of greaseproof (waxed) paper. If the cookies are iced or fragile, then shallow boxes that will hold the cookies in one or just a few layers are better than very deep ones.

Certain types of cookie can be individually wrapped in tissue paper or cellophane before packing into the box. Amaretti, for example, are usually wrapped in pairs in twists of fine tissue paper.

JARS, TINS AND OTHER CONTAINERS

Reusable containers such as glass or ceramic storage jars or tins, are more practical than simple cardboard boxes, as they have the advantage of being airtight. They also have the advantage of becoming part of the gift as well.

As well as packaging cookies in more conventional jars and tins, you could also consider packing cookies into a container such as a cup. Wrap the cookies in cellophane and tie with a ribbon, then place in the container. (This form of packaging is not airtight, so the cookies should be wrapped at the last minute.)

MAKING BOXES

It can be great fun making your own boxes or cartons to pack cookies in. It is also much cheaper than buying ready-made gift boxes, which can be surprisingly expensive. All you need is some fine cardboard, a metal ruler and a sharp knife.

MAKING A CUBE BOX

Following the template on the opposite page, draw the outline of the cube box on the back of a piece of coloured, patterned or plain cardboard. Cut out the shape and carefully score along the dotted lines with a sharp craft knife.

1 Fold along the dotted lines, sticking tab A to edge A (keeping the tab inside the box), then tab B to edge B. Repeat with tab C to edge C and tab D to edge D.

2 To create the lid, simply fold in tabs E and tuck the flap inside the box to hold the lid in place.

MAKING A CARTON

Following the template shown below, draw the outline of the carton on the back of a piece of fine cardboard and carefully cut out.

1 Score along the dotted lines using a sharp craft knife and cut out the four slots. You can use a hole punch to make the four holes as marked on the diagram.

2 Fold the carton along the scored lines, tucking tongue A into flaps B and tongue C into flaps D, so that the end of the tongue is on the inside of the carton. Fill the carton with cookies, then you can thread fine ribbon through the punched holes and tie together.

DECORATING BOXES

If you don't have time to make a box, you can cover a used box with coloured paper. Stick on gift wrap or coloured paper, then trim the paper back to the edges of the box.

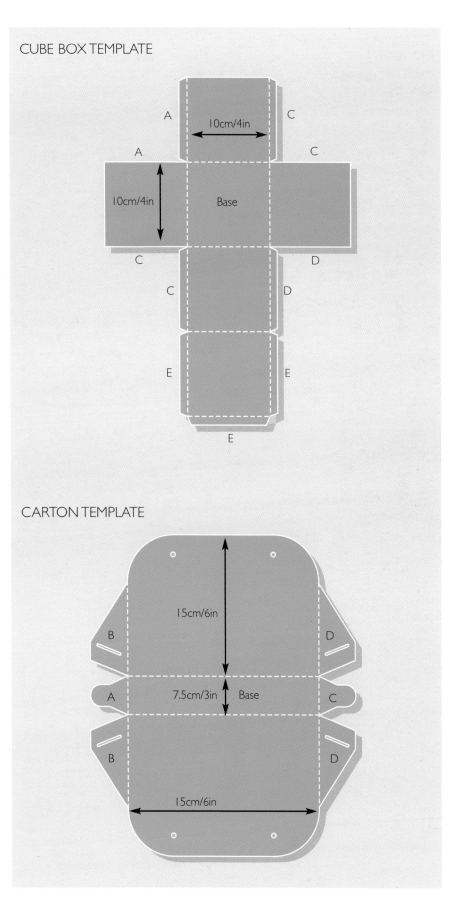

CUBE BOX TEMPLATE

A   10cm/4in   C
A   C
10cm/4in   Base
C   D
C   D
E   E
E

CARTON TEMPLATE

B   D
15cm/6in
A   7.5cm/3in   Base   C
B   D
15cm/6in

BAGS

You can buy pretty ready-made bags made out of paper, cardboard and cellophane, which look very attractive filled with cookies. Fabric bags can also look very pretty. Both are ideal for cookies that are to be given and eaten on the same day.

SIMPLE BAGS

These are best made from clear or coloured cellophane and make a perfect quick and easy wrapping for square or round cookies.

1 Cut a 25cm/10in square of cellophane. Put a pile of about six cookies in the centre.

2 Gather up the edges around the cookies, then tie a ribbon tightly where you've gathered the cellophane together. If you use curling ribbon, pull the ribbon between your thumb and the blade of a pair of scissors to create very pretty corkscrew curls.

POINTED BAGS

These are perfect for wrapping small cookies and long, thin fingers.

1 Cut a 40cm/16in square of cellophane. Fold it in quarters, hold the corner where the folds join and cut a quarter circle.

2 Open out and cut in half. Pull the two points of one half to meet. Slide one of the points behind the other to make a cone. Secure with sticky tape. Half-fill with cookies, then gather and tie with ribbon.

TUBE BAGS

These little packages, tied at both ends, are perfect for wrapping long, thin finger-shaped cookies such as brandy snaps. Simply cut out a sheet of cellophane that is about twice the length of the cookies, then roll a few cookies together to make a little tube-shaped package. Tie each end of the tube with ribbon to keep the cookies in place.

GIFT TAGS

Adding a label or gift tag to gift-wrapped cookies is the final touch. They can either carry a message or information about the ingredients and advice on storing. You can buy ready-made gift tags, make your own from thin cardboard or even bake your own individual cookie gift tags and ice on a message.

EDIBLE GIFT TAGS

These are pretty and fun, and make a really unusual, themed label.

1 Sift 75g/3oz/⅔ cup plain (all-purpose) flour, a pinch of bicarbonate of soda (baking soda) and a pinch of salt into a mixing bowl. Rub in 30g/1¼oz chilled, diced butter until the mixture resembles fine breadcrumbs. Stir in 40g/1½oz/ scant ¼ cup caster (superfine) sugar.

2 Blend together 15ml/1 tbsp golden (light corn) syrup and ½ egg yolk in a separate bowl. Add these to the dry ingredients and mix to a firm dough. Knead the dough lightly, then wrap in clear film (plastic wrap) and chill for 30 minutes.

3 Roll the dough out on a lightly floured surface to a thickness of 5mm/¼in, then stamp out gift tag-size shapes using a cookie cutter.

4 Using a skewer, pierce a hole for the ribbon to thread through about 1cm/½in from the top. Place the cookies on lightly greased baking sheets and bake in a preheated oven at 180°C/350°F/Gas 4 for 12–15 minutes, or until lightly browned. Leave on the baking sheets for 3 minutes, then, using a palette knife or metal spatula, transfer to a wire rack to cool.

5 Put a little royal icing – either white or coloured – in a paper piping (pastry) bag fitted with a writing nozzle. Pipe on your message, then leave the icing to dry. Thread ribbon through the holes made with the skewer and tie on to the cookies' container.

Cook's Tip
If the gift tag hole closes up during baking, gently pierce it again while the cookies are still hot. They will be too brittle once they have cooled.

SENDING COOKIES BY POST

If you choose cookies that are robust, there is no reason why you can't post your gift of cookies as long as you package them carefully and send by next-day delivery. Delicate iced cookies are not ideal for sending via post because they are too likely to be damaged.

1 Line the base and sides of a strong box or tin with bubble wrap or plenty of crumpled tissue paper to stop the cookies moving around.

2 Pack the cookies tightly into a box or tin, interleaving the layers with baking parchment.

3 Cut a piece of corrugated paper or bubblewrap and place between the cookies and the lid, then place the box in a plastic bag. (This will protect the cookies against damp or rain should the package be left on a doorstep or leaking mail box.)

4 Put the wrapped box in a slightly larger box, surrounded by more bubblewrap, foam pieces or crumpled paper to stop the two boxes knocking against each other.

5 Clearly address the package and label it fragile, then take the box to the post office immediately and send it next-day delivery.

Cook's Tip
It is not really practical to send home-made cookies abroad, as the mail is often unreliable and the arrival of stale cookies would be very disappointing for the recipient. In addition, some countries will have very strict rules about the importation and transportation of foodstuffs, even home-baked gifts, to protect their indigenous agriculture and to abide by local health and safety rules.

LISTING INGREDIENTS

When offering cookies as a gift, particularly when you do not give them in person, it is best to include information about the ingredients. Many people suffer from allergies and intolerance to certain foods, and many of the main food culprits are included in cookies. The most common being gluten in flour, dairy products in the form of butter, and eggs and nuts.

Even if you know the person to whom you are giving the cookies has no allergy, it is best to let them know what they contain in case they share them with someone who does have an allergy or intolerance.

Teatime Treats

Whether you are taking a well-earned five-minute break, entertaining friends for afternoon tea – a sadly forgotten custom these days – or attempting to stem the hunger pangs of ravenous children returning from school, this is the chapter to turn to. Tasty cookie treats range from Peanut Butter and Jelly Cookies, which are perfect for the kids, to Cappuccino Swirls – ideal for those with more sophisticated tastes.

Butter Cookies

These crunchy, buttery cookies make a delicious afternoon treat served with a cup of tea or a glass of milk. The dough can be made in advance and chilled until you are ready to bake the cookies.

Makes 25–30

175g/6oz/¾ cup unsalted (sweet) butter,
    at room temperature, diced
90g/3½oz/½ cup golden caster
    (superfine) sugar
250g/9oz/2¼ cups plain
    (all-purpose) flour
demerara (raw) sugar, for coating

1 Put the butter and sugar in a bowl and beat until light and fluffy. Add the flour and, using your hands, gradually work it in until the mixture forms a smooth dough. Roll into a sausage shape about 30cm/12in long, then pat the sides flat to form either a square or triangular log.

2 Sprinkle a thick layer of demerara sugar on a piece of greaseproof (waxed) paper. Press each side of the dough into the sugar to coat. Wrap and chill for about 30 minutes until firm. Meanwhile, preheat the oven to 160°C/325°F/Gas 3.

3 When ready to bake, remove the dough from the refrigerator and unwrap. Cut into thick slices and place slightly apart on non-stick baking sheets. Bake for 20 minutes until just beginning to turn brown. Transfer to a wire rack to cool.

Variations

• *To flavour the cookies, add ground cinnamon, grated lemon or orange rind, or vanilla or almond essence (extract) to the butter mixture, or add whole glacé (candied) cherries, chocolate chips, chopped nuts or dried fruit such as chopped apricots to the dough.*

• *As an alternative, coat the outside in granulated sugar or chopped toasted nuts.*

Peanut Butter and Jelly Cookies

These cookies are a twist on the original American peanut butter cookie and are a real hit with kids and adults alike. Give them a try – you'll love the crunchy nuts and sweet raspberry centres.

Makes 20–22

227g/8oz jar crunchy peanut butter
   (with no added sugar)

75g/3oz/6 tbsp unsalted (sweet) butter,
   at room temperature, diced

90g/3½oz/½ cup golden caster
   (superfine) sugar

50g/2oz/¼ cup light muscovado
   (brown) sugar

1 large (US extra large) egg, beaten

150g/5oz/1¼ cups self-raising
   (self-rising) flour

250g/9oz/scant 1 cup seedless
   raspberry jam

1 Preheat the oven to 180°C/350°F/ Gas 4. Line three or four baking sheets with baking parchment. Put the peanut butter and unsalted butter in a large bowl and beat together until well combined and creamy.

2 Add the caster and muscovado sugars and mix. Add the beaten egg and blend well. Sift in the flour and mix to a stiff dough.

3 Roll the dough into walnut-size balls between the palms of your hands. Place the balls on the prepared baking sheets and gently flatten each one with a fork to make a rough-textured cookie with a ridged surface. (Don't worry if the dough cracks slightly.)

4 Bake for 10–12 minutes, or until cooked but not browned. Using a palette knife (metal spatula), transfer to a wire rack to cool.

5 Spoon jam on to one cookie and top with a second. Continue to sandwich the cookies in this way.

Citrus Drops

These soft, cake-like treats are deliciously tangy, with a zesty, crumbly base filled with sweet, sticky lemon or orange curd. The crunchy topping of almonds makes the perfect finish.

Makes about 20
175g/6oz/¾ cup unsalted (sweet) butter,
  at room temperature, diced
150g/5oz/¾ cup caster
  (superfine) sugar
finely grated rind of 1 large lemon
finely grated rind of 1 orange
2 egg yolks
50g/2oz/½ cup ground almonds
225g/8oz/2 cups self-raising
  (self-rising) flour
lemon and/or orange curd
milk, for brushing
flaked (sliced) almonds,
  for sprinkling

1 Preheat the oven to 160°C/325°F/ Gas 3. Line two baking sheets with baking parchment. Beat the butter and sugar together until light and fluffy, then stir in the citrus rinds.

2 Stir the egg yolks into the mixture, then add the ground almonds and flour and mix well.

3 Divide the mixture into 20 pieces and shape into balls. Place on the baking sheets. Using the handle of a wooden spoon, make a hole in the centre of each cookie. Put 2.5ml/ ½ tsp lemon or orange curd into each hole and pinch the opening to semi-enclose the curd.

4 Brush the tops of each cookie with milk and sprinkle with flaked almonds. Bake for about 20 minutes until pale golden brown. Leave to cool slightly on the baking sheets to firm up, then transfer to a wire rack to cool completely.

Sugar-topped Vanilla Cookies

Buttery, crumbly vanilla cookies with an irresistible crunchy sugar topping, these are great with a cup of tea but also delicious served with luxury vanilla ice cream for a quick dessert.

Makes about 24

115g/4oz/½ cup unsalted (sweet) butter,
   at room temperature, diced
50g/2oz/¼ cup vanilla caster
   (superfine) sugar
1 egg, beaten
1.5ml/¼ tsp vanilla essence (extract)
200g/7oz/1¾ cups self-raising
   (self-rising) flour
45ml/3 tbsp cornflour (cornstarch)

For the topping

1 egg white
15ml/1 tbsp vanilla caster
   (superfine) sugar
75g/3oz sugar cubes, crushed

1 Preheat the oven to 180°C/350°F/ Gas 4. Put the butter and sugar in a bowl and beat until the mixture is light and fluffy. Beat in the egg and vanilla essence. Sift together the flour and cornflour over the mixture and mix to a soft but not sticky dough.

2 Roll the mixture out on a lightly floured surface. Using a flower biscuit (cookie) cutter or ring cutter, stamp out cookies and place on a non-stick baking sheet. Re-roll any trimmings and stamp out more cookies until you have used up all the dough.

3 For the topping, put the egg white in a small bowl and whisk until foamy. Whisk in the vanilla sugar. Using a pastry brush, spread generously on each cookie. Sprinkle with the crushed sugar cubes.

4 Bake for about 15 minutes, or until the topping is just beginning to turn golden brown. Remove from the oven and transfer to a wire rack to cool.

Cook's Tip

To make your own vanilla sugar, take a vanilla pod (bean) and split it open down one side. Place in a jar of sugar and use as necessary. If you don't have any vanilla sugar, increase the quantity of vanilla essence (extract) to 2.5ml/½ tsp.

Toffee Apple and Oat Crunchies

An unashamedly addictive mixture of chewy oats, soft apple and wonderfully crunchy toffee, this cookie won't win large prizes in the looks department but is top of the class for flavour.

Makes about 16

150g/5oz/10 tbsp unsalted
  (sweet) butter
175g/6oz/scant 1 cup light muscovado
  (brown) sugar
90g/3½oz/½ cup granulated sugar
1 large (US extra large) egg, beaten
75g/3oz/⅔ cup plain (all-purpose) flour
2.5ml/½ tsp bicarbonate of soda
  (baking soda)
pinch of salt
250g/9oz/2½ cups rolled oats
50g/2oz/scant ½ cup sultanas
  (golden raisins)
50g/2oz dried apple rings,
  coarsely chopped
50g/2oz chewy toffees, coarsely chopped

1 Preheat the oven to 180°C/350°F/ Gas 4. Line two or three baking sheets with baking parchment. In a large bowl, beat together the butter and both sugars until creamy. Add the beaten egg and stir well until thoroughly combined.

2 Sift together the flour, bicarbonate of soda and salt. Add to the butter, sugar and egg mixture and mix in well. Finally add the oats, sultanas, chopped apple rings and toffee pieces and stir gently until just combined.

3 Using a small ice cream scoop or large tablespoon, place heaps of the mixture well apart on the prepared baking sheets. Bake for about 10–12 minutes, or until lightly set in the centre and just beginning to brown at the edges.

4 Remove from the oven and leave to cool on the baking sheets for a few minutes. Using a palette knife (metal spatula), transfer the cookies to a wire rack to cool completely.

Apple and Elderflower Stars

These delicious, crumbly apple cookies are topped with a sweet yet very sharp icing. Packaged in a pretty box, they would make a delightfully festive gift for someone special.

Makes about 18

115g/4oz/½ cup unsalted (sweet) butter, at room temperature, diced

75g/3oz/scant ½ cup caster (superfine) sugar

2.5ml/½ tsp mixed (apple pie) spice

1 large (US extra large) egg yolk

25g/1oz dried apple rings, finely chopped

200g/7oz/1¾ cups self-raising (self-rising) flour

5–10ml/1–2 tsp milk, if necessary

For the topping

200g/7oz/1¾ cups icing (confectioners') sugar, sifted

60–90ml/4–6 tbsp elderflower cordial

granulated sugar, for sprinkling

1 Preheat the oven to 190°C/375°F/ Gas 5. Cream together the butter and sugar until light and fluffy. Beat in the mixed spice and egg yolk. Add the chopped apple and flour and stir together well. The mixture should form a stiff dough but if it is too dry, add some milk.

2 Roll the dough out on a floured surface to 5mm/¼in thick. Draw a five-pointed star on cardboard. Cut out and use as a template for the cookies. Alternatively, use a star biscuit (cookie) cutter.

3 Place the cookies on non-stick baking sheets and bake for about 10–15 minutes, or until just beginning to brown around the edges. Using a palette knife (metal spatula), carefully transfer the cookies to a wire rack to cool.

4 To make the topping, sift the icing sugar into a bowl and add just enough elderflower cordial to mix to a fairly thick but still pourable consistency.

5 When the cookies are completely cool, trickle the icing randomly over the stars. Immediately sprinkle with granulated sugar and leave to set.

Nutty Marshmallow and Chocolate Squares

Unashamedly sweet, with chocolate, marshmallows, cherries, nuts and coconut, this recipe is a favourite with children of all ages, and sweet-toothed adults too.

Makes 9

200g/7oz digestive biscuits
  (graham crackers)
90g/3½oz plain (semisweet) chocolate
200g/7oz mini coloured marshmallows
150g/5oz/1¼ cups chopped walnuts
90g/3½oz/scant ½ cup glacé (candied)
  cherries, halved
50g/2oz/⅔ cup sweetened desiccated
  (dry shredded) coconut
350g/12oz milk chocolate

1 Put the digestive biscuits in a polythene bag and, using a rolling pin, crush them until they are fairly small. Place them in a bowl. Melt the plain chocolate in the microwave or in a heatproof bowl set over a pan of hot water. Pour the melted plain chocolate over the broken biscuits and stir well. Spread the mixture in the base of a 20cm/8in square shallow cake tin (pan).

2 Put the marshmallows, walnuts, cherries and coconut in a large bowl. Melt the milk chocolate in the microwave or in a heatproof bowl set over a pan of hot water.

3 Pour the melted milk chocolate over the marshmallow and nut mixture and toss gently together until almost everything is coated. Spread the mixture over the chocolate base, but leave in chunky lumps – do not spread flat.

4 Chill until set, then cut into squares or bars.

Variation

Other nuts can be used instead of the walnuts – the choice is yours.

Almond-scented Chocolate Cherry Wedges

These cookies are a chocoholic's dream, and use the very best quality chocolate. Erratically shaped, they are packed with crunchy cookies, juicy raisins and munchy nuts.

Makes about 15

50g/2oz ratafia biscuits (almond macaroons) or small amaretti

90g/3½oz shortcake biscuits (cookies)

150g/5oz/1 cup jumbo raisins

50g/2oz/¼ cup undyed glacé (candied) cherries, quartered

450g/1lb dark (bittersweet) chocolate (minimum 70 per cent cocoa solids)

90g/3½oz/scant ½ cup unsalted (sweet) butter, diced

30ml/2 tbsp amaretto liqueur (optional)

25g/1oz/¼ cup toasted flaked (sliced) almonds

1 Line a baking sheet with baking parchment. Put the ratafia biscuits or amaretti in a large bowl. Leave half whole and break the remainder into coarse pieces. Break each of the shortcake biscuits into three or four jagged pieces and add to the bowl. Add the raisins and cherries and toss lightly together.

Cook's Tip

If you cannot find undyed glacé cherries in the supermarket, look for them in your local delicatessen instead.

2 Melt the chocolate and butter with the liqueur, if using, in the microwave or in a heatproof bowl set over a pan of hot water. When the chocolate has melted, remove from the heat and stir the mixture until combined and smooth. Set aside to cool slightly.

3 Pour the chocolate over the biscuit mixture and toss lightly together until everything is coated in chocolate. Spread out over the prepared baking sheet. Sprinkle over the almonds and push them in at angles so they stick well to the chocolate-coated biscuits.

4 When the mixture is completely cold and set, cut or break into crazy shapes, as you wish, such as long thin triangles, short stumpy squares or irregular shapes.

Ginger Cookies

These are a supreme treat for ginger lovers – richly spiced cookies packed with chunks of succulent preserved stem ginger.

Makes 30 small or 20 large cookies

350g/12oz/3 cups self-raising
  (self-rising) flour
pinch of salt
200g/7oz/1 cup golden caster
  (superfine) sugar
15ml/1 tbsp ground ginger
5ml/1 tsp bicarbonate of soda
  (baking soda)
115g/4oz/½ cup unsalted (sweet) butter
90g/3½oz/generous ¼ cup golden
  (light corn) syrup
1 large (US extra large) egg, beaten
150g/5oz preserved stem ginger in syrup,
  drained and coarsely chopped

1 Preheat the oven to 160°C/325°F/ Gas 3. Line three baking sheets with baking parchment or lightly greased greaseproof (waxed) paper.

2 Sift the flour into a large mixing bowl, add the salt, caster sugar, ground ginger and bicarbonate of soda and stir to combine.

3 Dice the butter and put it in a small, heavy pan with the syrup. Heat gently, stirring, until the butter has melted. Remove from the heat and set aside to cool until just warm.

4 Pour the butter mixture over the dry ingredients, then add the egg and two-thirds of the ginger. Mix thoroughly, then use your hands to bring the dough together.

5 Shape the dough into 20 large or 30 small balls, depending on the size you require. Place them, spaced well apart, on the baking sheets.

6 Gently flatten the balls, then press a few pieces of the remaining preserved stem ginger into the top of each of the cookies.

7 Bake for about 12–15 minutes, depending on the size of your cookies, until light golden in colour. Remove from the oven and leave to cool for 1 minute on the baking sheets to firm up. Using a palette knife (metal spatula), transfer to a wire rack to cool completely.

Fig and Date Ravioli

These melt-in-the-mouth cushions of sweet pastry are filled with a delicious mixture of figs, dates and walnuts and dusted with icing sugar. They are ideal for serving with tea or coffee.

Makes about 20

375g/13oz packet sweet
  shortcrust pastry
milk, for brushing
icing (confectioners') sugar, sifted,
  for dusting

For the filling

115g/4oz/²⁄₃ cup ready-to-eat dried figs
50g/2oz/⅓ cup stoned (pitted) dates
15g/½oz/1 tbsp chopped walnuts
10ml/2 tsp lemon juice
15ml/1 tbsp clear honey

1 Preheat the oven to 180°C/350°F/ Gas 4. To make the filling, put all the ingredients into a food processor and blend to a paste.

2 Roll out just under half of the shortcrust pastry on a lightly floured surface to a square. Place spoonfuls of the fig paste on the pastry in neat rows at equally spaced intervals, as when making ravioli.

3 Roll out the remaining pastry to a slightly larger square. Dampen all around each spoonful of filling, using a pastry brush dipped in cold water. Place the second sheet of pastry on top and press together around each mound of filling.

4 Using a zigzag pastry wheel or a pizza cutter, cut squares between the mounds of filling. Place the cookies on non-stick baking sheets and lightly brush the top of each with a little milk. Bake for 15–20 minutes until golden.

5 Using a palette knife (metal spatula), transfer the cookies to a wire rack to cool. When cool, dust with icing sugar.

Coconut and Lime Macaroons

These pretty pistachio nut topped cookies are crunchy on the outside and soft and gooey in the centre. The zesty lime topping contrasts wonderfully with the sweet coconut.

Makes 12–14

4 large (US extra large) egg whites
250g/9oz/3 cups sweetened desiccated (dry shredded) coconut
150g/5oz/¾ cup granulated sugar
10ml/2 tsp vanilla essence (extract)
25g/1oz/¼ cup plain (all-purpose) flour
115g/4oz/1 cup icing (confectioners') sugar, sifted
grated rind of 1 lime
15–20ml/3–4 tsp lime juice
about 15g/½oz/1 tbsp pistachio nuts, chopped

1 Preheat the oven to 180°C/350°F/Gas 4. Line two baking sheets with baking parchment. Put the egg whites, desiccated coconut, sugar, vanilla essence and flour in a large, heavy pan. Mix well.

2 Place over a low heat and cook for 6–8 minutes, stirring constantly to ensure it does not stick. When the mixture becomes the consistency of thick porridge (oatmeal), remove from the heat.

3 Place spoonfuls of the mixture in rocky piles on the lined baking sheets. Bake for 12–13 minutes, until golden brown. Remove from the oven and leave to cool completely on the baking sheets.

4 To make the topping, put the icing sugar and lime rind into a bowl and add enough lime juice to give a thick pouring consistency. Place a spoonful of icing on each macaroon and allow it to drip down the sides. Sprinkle over the pistachio nuts and serve.

Variation
If you prefer, make Coconut and Lemon Macaroons by substituting grated lemon rind and juice.

Cappuccino Swirls

A melt-in-the-mouth, mocha-flavoured cookie drizzled with white and dark chocolate is just the thing to have with that mid-morning caffè latte, as well as with afternoon tea with friends.

Makes 18

10ml/2 tsp instant coffee powder
10ml/2 tsp boiling water
150g/5oz/1¼ cups plain
   (all-purpose) flour
115g/4oz/½ cup cornflour (cornstarch)
15ml/1 tbsp (unsweetened) cocoa
   powder
225g/8oz/1 cup unsalted (sweet) butter,
   at room temperature, diced
50g/2oz/¼ cup golden caster
   (superfine) sugar

For the decoration

50g/2oz white chocolate
25g/1oz dark (bittersweet) chocolate

1 Preheat the oven to 190°C/375°F/ Gas 5. Line two baking sheets with baking parchment. Put the coffee powder in a cup, add the boiling water and stir until dissolved. Set aside to cool. Sift together the flour, cornflour and cocoa powder.

2 Put the butter and sugar in a bowl and beat until creamy. Add the coffee and the sifted flour and mix well. Spoon into a piping (pastry) bag fitted with a plain nozzle.

3 Pipe 18 spirals, slightly apart, on to the prepared baking sheets.

4 Bake for 10–15 minutes, or until firm but not browned. Remove from the oven and leave on the baking sheets for 1 minute, then transfer to a wire rack to cool.

5 Melt the white and dark chocolate separately in heatproof bowls set over a pan of hot water.

6 Place the cooled cookies close together on kitchen paper. Using a teaspoon, take some white chocolate and flick over the cookies, moving your hand speedily from left to right to create small lines of chocolate drizzle over them.

7 When all the white chocolate has been used, repeat the process with the dark chocolate, flicking it over the cookies so the dark chocolate is at an angle to the white chocolate. Leave until the chocolate has set and then remove the cookies from the paper.

Celebration Cookies

Food and festivals go together – from China to America and from January to December, you cannot have a celebration without cooking something special to eat. Of course, you don't have to wait for Diwali to enjoy Neuris, Hanukkah to feast on Rugelach or Easter to bake a batch of Simnel Cookies. Making any of the cookies in this chapter will turn an ordinary day into a special occasion and an international celebration.

Spicy Hearts and Stars

These soft, sweet cookies have a wonderfully chewy texture and a deliciously warm, fragrant flavour. Serve with coffee at the end of a festive meal, or make them as a gift on a special occasion.

Makes about 25

115g/4oz/½ cup unsalted (sweet)
  butter, softened
115g/4oz/generous ½ cup light
  muscovado (brown) sugar
1 egg
50g/2oz/1½ tbsp golden
  (light corn) syrup
50g/2oz/1½ tbsp black treacle
  (molasses)
400g/14oz/3½ cups self-raising
  (self-rising) flour
10ml/2 tsp ground ginger

For the toppings

200g/7oz plain (semisweet) or
  milk chocolate
150g/5oz/1¼ cups icing (confectioners')
  sugar, sifted

1 Beat together the butter and sugar until creamy. Beat in the egg, syrup and treacle together. Sift in the flour and ginger and mix to form a firm dough. Chill for 20 minutes. Meanwhile, preheat the oven to 180°C/350°F/Gas 4 and line two large baking sheets with a layer of baking parchment.

2 Roll out the dough on a lightly floured surface to just under 1cm/½ in thick and use biscuit (cookie) cutters to stamp out heart and star shapes. Place, spaced slightly apart, on the prepared baking sheets and bake for about 10 minutes, or until risen. Cool on a wire rack.

3 To make the toppings, melt the chocolate in a microwave or in a heatproof bowl set over a pan of barely simmering water. Use the melted chocolate to coat the heart-shaped cookies. Put the icing sugar into a bowl and mix with enough warm water to make a coating consistency, then use this to glaze the star-shaped cookies.

Kourabiedes

Lightly spiced and delicately flavoured with orange flower water and almonds, these crisp little crescents are perfect for parties and festive occasions such as christenings and weddings.

Makes about 20

115g/4oz/½ cup unsalted (sweet) butter, softened
pinch of ground nutmeg
10ml/2 tsp orange flower water
50g/2oz/½ cup icing (confectioners') sugar, plus extra for dusting
90g/3½oz/¾ cup plain (all-purpose) flour
115g/4oz/1 cup ground almonds
25g/1oz/¼ cup whole almonds, toasted and chopped

1 Preheat the oven to 160°C/325°F/ Gas 3. Line two large baking sheets with baking parchment. Beat the butter in a large bowl until soft and creamy.

2 Beat in the nutmeg and orange flower water. Add the icing sugar and beat until fluffy.

3 Add the flour, ground and chopped almonds and mix well, then use your hands to bring the mixture together to form a dough, being careful not to overwork it.

4 Shape pieces of dough into sausages about 7.5cm/3in long. Curve each one into a crescent shape and place, spaced well apart, on the prepared baking sheets. Bake for about 15 minutes, or until firm but still pale in colour. Cool for about 5 minutes, then dust with a little icing sugar.

Christmas Tree Angels

Why not make these charming edible decorations to brighten your Yuletide? However, don't hang them on the tree until Christmas Eve or they'll all be gone by Christmas Day.

Makes 20–30
90g/3½oz/scant ½ cup demerara
   (raw) sugar
200g/7oz/scant1 cup golden
   (light corn) syrup
5ml/1 tsp ground ginger
5ml/1 tsp ground cinnamon
1.5ml/¼ tsp ground cloves
115g/4oz/½ cup unsalted (sweet) butter,
   cut into pieces
10ml/2 tsp bicarbonate of soda
   (baking soda)
1 egg, beaten
500g/1¼lb/4½ cups plain (all-purpose)
   flour, sifted

For the decoration
1 egg white
175–225g/6–8oz/1½–2 cups icing
   (confectioners') sugar, sifted
silver and gold balls
fine ribbon

1 Preheat the oven to 160°C/325°F/ Gas 3. Line two large baking sheets with baking parchment. Put the sugar, syrup, ginger, cinnamon and cloves into a heavy pan and bring to the boil over a low heat, stirring constantly. Once the mixture has boiled, remove the pan from the heat.

2 Put the pieces of butter in a large heatproof bowl and pour over the hot sugar and syrup mixture. Add the bicarbonate of soda and stir well until the butter has completely melted. Beat the egg into the mixture, then stir in the flour. Mix thoroughly and then knead to form a smooth dough.

3 Divide the dough into four pieces and roll out, one at a time, between sheets of baking parchment, to a thickness of about 3mm/⅛in. Keep the unrolled dough in a polythene bag until needed to prevent it from drying out. Stamp out festive shapes, such as Christmas trees, using biscuit (cookie) cutters, or make angels, as follows.

4 To make simple angels, stamp out rounds of dough of any size you like, using a plain cutter. Don't make them too big or they might be too heavy to hang on the Christmas tree. As shown in the photograph, cut off two segments from either side of the round to give a body and two wings. Place the wings, rounded side facing down, behind the body and press lightly together with your fingers.

5 Roll a small piece of dough for the head, place at the top of the body and flatten with your fingers. Using a skewer, make a wide hole in the cookies through which ribbon can be threaded when they are cooked. Place on the baking sheets. Bake the cookies for 10–15 minutes until golden brown. Transfer to a wire rack to cool.

6 To make the decoration, beat the egg white with a fork. Whisk in icing sugar until you have an icing of soft-peak consistency.

7 Put the icing in a piping (pastry) bag fitted with a plain writing nozzle and decorate the cookies with simple designs. Add silver and gold balls before the icing has set. Finally, thread fine ribbon through the holes in the cookies.

Speculaas

These Dutch cookies are made from a spicy dough wrapped around a wonderfully rich marzipan filling. They are eaten in Holland around the Feast of St Nicholas on 6 December.

Makes about 35

175g/6oz/1½ cups ground hazelnuts
175g/6oz/1½ cups ground almonds
175g/6oz/scant 1 cup caster
 (superfine) sugar
175g/6oz/1½ cups icing
 (confectioners') sugar
1 egg, beaten
10–15ml/2–3 tsp lemon juice
250g/9oz/2¼ cups self-raising
 (self-rising) flour
5ml/1 tsp mixed (apple pie) spice
75g/3oz/⅓ cup light muscovado
 (brown) sugar
115g/4oz/½ cup unsalted (sweet) butter,
 at room temperature, diced
2 eggs
15ml/1 tbsp milk
15ml/1 tbsp caster (superfine) sugar
about 35 blanched almond halves

1 For the filling, put the ground hazelnuts, almonds, caster sugar, icing sugar, beaten egg and 10ml/2 tsp lemon juice in a bowl and mix to a firm paste, adding more lemon juice if needed. Divide the mixture in half and roll each piece into a sausage shape about 25cm/10in long. Wrap in clear film (plastic wrap) and chill in the refrigerator.

2 To make the dough, sift the flour and mixed spice into a large mixing bowl then stir in the muscovado sugar. Add the butter and rub in well with your fingertips.

3 Beat one of the eggs, add to the mixture and mix together to form a dough. Knead lightly, then wrap in clear film and chill in the refrigerator for 15 minutes. Meanwhile, preheat the oven to 180°C/350°F/Gas 4 and line a large baking sheet with baking parchment.

4 Roll out the pastry on a lightly floured surface to a 30cm/12in square and cut in half to make two equal rectangles. Beat the remaining egg and brush some all over the pastry rectangles.

5 Place a roll of filling on each piece of pastry and roll the pastry to enclose the filling. Place, join side down, on the baking sheet.

6 Beat the remains of the egg with the milk and caster sugar and brush over the rolls. Press almond halves along the top. Bake for 35 minutes until golden brown. Leave to cool before cutting diagonally into slices.

Sweet Hearts

These cookies are for Valentine's Day or an anniversary, but you could use different-shaped cutters in the same way to make cookies for other occasions – stars and bells for Christmas, perhaps, or fluted "flowers" for a special birthday or Mother's Day present.

Makes 12–14

50g/2oz/¼ cup unsalted (sweet)
* butter, softened*
75g/3oz/scant ½ cup caster (superfine) sugar
1 egg yolk
150g/5oz/1¼ cups plain (all-purpose) flour
25g/1oz dark (bittersweet) chocolate,
* melted and cooled*
25–50g/1–2oz dark (bittersweet)
* chocolate, to decorate*

1 Preheat the oven to 180°C/350°F/ Gas 4. Line two baking sheets with baking parchment. Put the butter, sugar and egg yolk in a mixing bowl and beat well. Stir in the flour and then knead until smooth.

2 Divide the dough in half, then knead the melted chocolate into one half until it is evenly coloured.

3 Roll out the chocolate dough between two sheets of baking parchment, to a thickness of about 3mm/⅛in. Then roll out the plain dough in the same way.

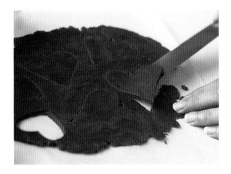

4 Cut out hearts from both doughs using a 7.5cm/3in biscuit (cookie) cutter. Place the hearts on the prepared baking sheets.

5 Using a smaller heart-shaped cutter, stamp out the centres from all the hearts. Place a light-coloured heart in the centre of a larger chocolate heart and vice versa.

6 Bake the cookies for about 10 minutes, or until just beginning to turn brown. Remove from the oven and leave to cool.

7 To decorate, melt the chocolate in a microwave or in a heatproof bowl set over a pan of hot water. Put into a disposable piping (pastry) bag. Leave the chocolate to cool slightly.

8 Snip the end off the piping bag and carefully pipe dots directly onto the outer part of the large chocolate hearts (with the plain centres). Then pipe zigzags on the pale part of the large plain hearts (with the chocolate centres). Put the cookies aside in a cool place and leave until they are set.

Variation
For a tasty variation, make chocolate and orange hearts by kneading 10ml/2 tsp very finely grated orange rind into the plain dough.

Fourth of July Blueberry Softbakes

These are simply wonderful when eaten still warm from the oven. However, they are also good if allowed to cool and then packed for a traditional Independence Day picnic.

Makes 10

150g/5oz/1¼ cups plain
   (all-purpose) flour
7.5ml/1½ tsp baking powder
5ml/1 tsp ground cinnamon
50g/2oz/¼ cup unsalted (sweet) butter,
   at room temperature, diced
50g/2oz/¼ cup demerara (raw) sugar,
   plus extra for sprinkling
120ml/4fl oz/½ cup sour cream
90g/3½oz/1 cup fresh blueberries
50g/2oz/½ cup semi-dried cranberries

Variation

For Hallowe'en or Thanksgiving, substitute fresh cranberries for the blueberries and chopped preserved stem ginger for the semi-dried cranberries.

1 Preheat the oven to 190°C/375°F/ Gas 5. Line two baking sheets with baking parchment. Sift together the flour, baking powder and cinnamon into a large mixing bowl. Add the diced butter and rub in with your fingers until the mixture resembles fine breadcrumbs. Stir in the demerara sugar.

2 Add the sour cream, blueberries and cranberries and stir until just combined. Spoon ten mounds of the mixture, spaced well apart, on to the prepared baking sheets. Sprinkle with the extra demerara sugar and bake for about 20 minutes, or until golden and firm in the centre. Serve warm.

Simnel Cookies

Enjoy these mini variations on the sweet, marzipan-covered simnel cake that is traditionally eaten at Easter and, originally, Mothering Sunday in Britain. Children will enjoy decorating them.

Makes about 18

175g/6oz/¾ cup unsalted (sweet) butter, at room temperature, diced
115g/4oz/generous ½ cup caster (superfine) sugar
finely grated rind of 1 lemon
2 egg yolks
225g/8oz/2 cups plain (all-purpose) flour
50g/2oz/¼ cup currants

For the topping

400g/14oz/¾ cup marzipan
200g/7oz/1¾ cups icing (confectioners') sugar, sifted
2–3 shades of food colouring
mini sugar-coated chocolate Easter eggs

1 Preheat the oven to 180°C/350°F/Gas 4. Put the butter, sugar and lemon rind in a bowl and cream with a wooden spoon or electric mixer until light and fluffy. Beat in the egg yolks, then stir in the flour and currants and mix to a firm dough. If it is a little soft, chill in the refrigerator until firm.

2 Roll the dough out on a sheet of baking parchment to just under 5mm/¼in thickness. Using a 9cm/3½in fluted cutter, stamp out rounds and place, spaced slightly apart, on two non-stick baking sheets.

3 To make the topping, roll out the marzipan to just under 5mm/¼in thickness and use a 6cm/2½in plain or fluted cutter to stamp out the same number of rounds as there are cookies. Place a marzipan round on top of each cookie and press down very gently to fix the marzipan to the cookie dough.

4 Bake the cookies for about 12 minutes, or until just golden. Remove from the oven and leave to cool on the baking sheets.

5 Put the icing sugar in a bowl and add just enough water to mix to a smooth, soft, spreadable consistency. Divide the icing among two or three bowls and add a few drops of different food colouring to each one. Stir until evenly mixed.

6 Divide the cooled cookies into three batches and spread each batch with icing of a different colour. While the icing is still wet, gently press a few sugar-coated eggs on top of each cookie and leave to set.

Rugelach

Jewish cookies, traditionally served during the eight-day festival of Hanukkah, these little crescents have a spicy fruit-and-nut filling. They can be enjoyed at any time of the year.

3 Divide the dough into four. Take one piece and leave the rest in the refrigerator, as it is important to keep the dough as cold as possible because it is very sticky and therefore difficult to roll out. Sprinkle a sheet of baking parchment with flour and quickly roll out the dough to a round as thin as possible. Cut into six wedges; sprinkle with a quarter of the filling.

4 Starting at the wide end, roll each triangle up towards the point. Curve each roll into a crescent and place, the pointed side down, on the prepared baking sheets. Repeat with the remaining dough and filling.

5 Brush with beaten egg and bake for about 15–20 minutes, or until golden brown. Transfer to a wire rack and leave to cool.

Makes about 24

115g/4oz/½ cup unsalted (sweet) butter, chilled and diced
115g/4oz/½ cup cream cheese
120ml/4fl oz/½ cup sour cream
250g/9oz/2¼ cups plain (all-purpose) flour
beaten egg, to glaze

For the filling

50g/2oz/¼ cup caster (superfine) sugar
10ml/2 tsp ground cinnamon
60ml/4 tbsp raisins, chopped
60ml/4 tbsp ready-to-eat dried apricots, chopped
75g/3oz/¾ cup walnuts, finely chopped

1 To make the dough, put the butter, cream cheese and sour cream into a food processor and process until just creamy and combined. Add the flour and process briefly, using the pulse button, until the mixture just comes together, taking care not to overmix. Remove, wrap in clear film (plastic wrap) and chill for at least 6 hours.

2 Preheat the oven to 180°C/350°F/ Gas 4. Line two large baking sheets with baking parchment. To make the filling, put all the filling ingredients in a bowl and mix until thoroughly combined.

Oznei Haman

These little cookies, shaped like tricorns – three-cornered hats – are eaten at the Jewish feast called Purim, which celebrates the Jews' deliverance from the scheming Haman.

Makes about 20

115g/4oz/½ cup unsalted (sweet) butter, at room temperature, diced
115g/4oz/generous ½ cup caster (superfine) sugar
2.5ml/½ tsp vanilla essence (extract)
3 egg yolks
250g/9oz/2¼ cups plain (all-purpose) flour
beaten egg to seal and glaze

For the filling

40g/1½oz/3 tbsp poppy seeds
15ml/1 tbsp clear honey
25g/1oz/2 tbsp caster (superfine) sugar
finely grated rind of 1 lemon
15ml/1 tbsp lemon juice
40g/1½oz/⅓ cup ground almonds
1 small (US medium) egg, beaten
25g/1oz/scant ¼ cup raisins

1 Beat the butter with the sugar until light and creamy. Beat in the vanilla and egg yolks. Sift over the flour, stir in, then work into a dough with your hands. Knead until smooth. Wrap in clear film (plastic wrap) and chill.

2 For the filling, put the poppy seeds, honey, sugar, lemon rind and juice into a pan with 60ml/4 tbsp water and bring to the boil, stirring. Remove from the heat and beat in the almonds, egg and raisins. Cool.

3 Preheat the oven to 180°C/350°F/ Gas 4. Line two large baking sheets with baking parchment. Roll out the dough on a lightly floured surface to 3mm/⅛in thickness. Using a plain round 7.5cm/3in cutter, stamp out rounds. Place a heaped teaspoon of filling on each round. Brush the edges with beaten egg, then bring the sides to the centre to form a tricorne shape. Seal the edges well together and place on the prepared baking sheets, spaced slightly apart.

4 Brush with beaten egg and bake for 20–30 minutes, or until golden brown. Transfer to a wire rack and leave to cool.

Chinese Fortune Cookies

Whether you're a rabbit or a dragon, a snake or a tiger, these charming cookies are sure to delight and are a wonderful way to celebrate the Chinese New Year with family and friends.

Makes about 35

2 egg whites
50g/2oz/½ cup icing (confectioner's)
   sugar, sifted, plus extra for dusting
5ml/1 tsp almond or vanilla
   essence (extract)
25g/1oz/2 tbsp unsalted (sweet)
   butter, melted
50g/2oz/½ cup plain (all-purpose) flour
25g/1oz/⅓ cup desiccated (dry
   unsweetened shredded) coconut,
   lightly toasted
tiny strips of paper with "good luck",
   "health, wealth and happiness" and
   other appropriate messages typed or
   written on them, to decorate

1 Preheat the oven to 190°C/375°F/ Gas 5. Prepare two or three sheets of baking parchment (they can be used more than once) by cutting them to the size of a baking sheet. Draw two or three circles of about 7.5cm/3in diameter, with a little distance between them, on each sheet of parchment. Place one of these sheets of parchment on the baking sheet and set aside.

2 Put the egg whites into a clean, grease-free bowl and whisk until foamy and white. Whisk in the icing sugar, a little at a time. Beat in the almond or vanilla essence and the butter. Stir in the flour and mix lightly until smooth.

Cook's Tip

You need to work quickly to shape the cookies. Placing the hot cookies on the rim of wine glasses sets them with a curve in the centre.

3 Place a teaspoonful of mixture into the centre of each marked circle on the prepared parchment and spread out evenly to fit the circle. Sprinkle with a little coconut. Bake one sheet at a time (as you will only have enough time to shape one sheetful of cookies before they set) for about 5 minutes, or until very lightly brown on the edges.

4 Remove the cookies from the oven, immediately loosely fold in half and place on the rim of a glass. Leave until firm, then transfer to a wire rack. Continue baking one sheet of cookies at a time.

5 Tuck the messages into the side of each cookie. Dust very lightly with icing sugar before serving.

Neuris

These melt-in-the-mouth sweet and spicy samosas are traditionally eaten during the Hindu festival of Diwali and are also given as little gifts to friends and family at this time.

Makes 12

75g/3oz/1 cup desiccated (dry
    unsweetened shredded) coconut
50g/2oz/¼ cup light muscovado
    (brown) sugar
25g/1oz/¼ cup cashew nuts, chopped
50g/2oz/⅓ cup seedless raisins
250ml/8fl oz/1 cup evaporated
    (unsweetened condensed) milk
large pinch grated nutmeg
2.5ml/½ tsp ground cinnamon
12 sheets filo pastry, about 28 x 18cm/
    11 x 7in each
sunflower oil, for brushing

For the topping

15ml/1 tbsp evaporated (unsweetened
    condensed) milk
15ml/1 tbsp caster (superfine) sugar
desiccated coconut

1 To make the filling, put the coconut, muscovado sugar, cashews, raisins and evaporated milk into a small pan. Bring to the boil, stirring occasionally. Reduce the heat to very low and cook for about 10 minutes, stirring, until the milk has been absorbed. Stir in the nutmeg and cinnamon, then set aside to cool.

2 Preheat the oven to 180°C/350°F/ Gas 4. Line two baking sheets with baking parchment.

3 Brush one sheet of filo pastry with a little sunflower oil. Fold the sheet in half lengthways, then brush with more oil and fold widthways. Brush the edges of the folded pastry with water.

4 Place a spoonful of the cooled filling on one half of the folded pastry sheet. Fold the other half of the sheet over the filling, then press together the edges to seal. Trim off the rough edges and place on the baking sheet. Continue making neuris in this way until all the pastry and filling has been used up.

5 To make the topping, put the evaporated milk and sugar into a small pan and heat gently, stirring constantly until the sugar has completely dissolved.

6 Brush the topping over the neuris and sprinkle them with the coconut. Bake for about 20 minutes, until crisp and golden brown. Transfer to a wire rack and leave to cool before serving.

Wholesome Bites

When anyone is trying to lose weight or eat a healthier diet, the first items to be scrapped are almost always cookies, but this doesn't have to be the case. The recipes in this chapter are nutritious and delicious, packed with fruit, fibre and flavour. Many are low in fat and use natural sweeteners rather than refined sugars. You don't even have to sacrifice "chocolate" cookies. They are the perfect pick-me-up for adults and ideal for after-school snacks.

Low-fat Orange Oaties

These are so delicious that it is difficult to believe that they are healthy too. As they are packed with flavour and wonderfully crunchy, the whole family will love them.

Makes about 16

175g/6oz/¾ cup clear honey
120ml/4fl oz/½ cup orange juice
90g/3½oz/1 cup rolled oats,
   lightly toasted
115g/4oz/1 cup plain (all-purpose) flour
115g/4oz/generous ½ cup golden caster
   (superfine) sugar
finely grated rind of 1 orange
5ml/1 tsp bicarbonate of soda
   (baking soda)

1 Preheat the oven to 180°C/350°F/ Gas 4. Line two baking sheets with baking parchment.

2 Put the honey and orange juice in a small pan and simmer over a low heat for 8–10 minutes, stirring occasionally, until the mixture is thick and syrupy.

3 Put the oats, flour, sugar and orange rind into a bowl. Mix the bicarbonate of soda with 15ml/ 1 tbsp boiling water and add to the flour mixture, together with the honey and orange syrup. Mix well with a wooden spoon.

4 Place spoonfuls of the mixture on to the prepared baking sheets, spaced slightly apart, and bake for 10–12 minutes, or until golden brown. Leave to cool on the sheets for 5 minutes before transferring to a wire rack to cool completely.

Luxury Muesli Cookies

It is best to use a "luxury" muesli for this recipe, preferably one with 50 per cent mixed cereal and 50 per cent fruit, nuts and seeds. These buttery, crunchy cookies are ideal for a snack at any time.

Makes about 20

115g/4oz/½ cup unsalted (sweet) butter
45ml/3 tbsp golden (light corn) syrup
115g/4oz/generous ½ cup demerara
  (raw) sugar
175g/6oz/1½ cups "luxury" muesli (granola)
90g/3½oz/¾ cup self-raising (self-rising) flour
5ml/1 tsp ground cinnamon

1 Preheat the oven to 160°C/325°F/ Gas 3. Line two or three baking sheets with baking parchment.

Variation
Tropical muesli containing coconut and dried tropical fruits makes an interesting alternative to regular luxury muesli.

2 Put the butter, syrup and sugar in a large pan and heat gently. Stir constantly until the butter has completely melted. Remove the pan from the heat then stir in the muesli, flour and cinnamon and mix together well. Set aside to cool slightly.

3 Place spoonfuls of the mixture, slightly apart, on the baking sheets. Bake for 15 minutes until the cookies are just beginning to brown around the edges. Leave to cool for a few minutes on the baking sheets, then carefully transfer to a wire rack to cool completely.

Ker-runch Cookies

An unusual coating of bran flakes covers these small cookies – a painless way of making sure that you have plenty of fibre in your diet. They are fun to make too.

Makes about 18

175g/6oz/¾ cup vegetable margarine
175g/6oz/¾ cup light muscovado
  (brown) sugar
1 egg
175g/6oz/1½ cups self-raising
  (self-rising) wholemeal
  (whole-wheat) flour
115g/4oz/generous 1 cup rolled oats
115g/4oz/⅔ cup mixed dried fruit
50g/2oz/2 cups bran flakes
  breakfast cereal

1 Preheat the oven to 160°C/325°F/ Gas 3. Line two baking sheets with baking parchment. Put the margarine and sugar in a bowl and beat until pale and creamy.

2 Add the egg to the margarine mixture and beat in until thoroughly combined. Stir in the flour, oats and fruit. Roll into walnut-size balls between the palms of your hands. Spread out the bran flakes on a shallow plate and roll the balls in them to coat.

3 Place on the prepared baking sheets and flatten each one gently with your hand.

4 Bake for about 20 minutes until firm and golden brown. Remove from the baking sheets while still hot as these cookies firm up very quickly. Place on a wire rack to cool.

Iced Carob Cookies

If you are unable to eat chocolate but still crave it, these heavenly cookies, with their creamy topping, provide the answer to your prayers.

Makes 12–16

115g/4oz/½ cup butter

10ml/2 tsp carob powder

115g/4oz/1 cup wholemeal (whole-wheat) flour

5ml/1 tsp baking powder

75g/3oz/⅓ cup muscovado (molasses) sugar

50g/2oz/generous ½ cup rolled oats

For the topping

50g/2oz carob bar, coarsely chopped

45ml/3 tbsp double (heavy) cream

15ml/1 tbsp chopped ready-to-eat dried apricots

Cook's Tip

Carob is derived from the carob bean, which has a nutritious, flavoursome pulp.

1 Preheat the oven to 190°C/375°F/ Gas 5. Line the base and sides of an 18cm/7in square shallow cake tin (pan) with baking parchment. Put the butter in a large pan and add the carob powder. Stir over a low heat until the mixture is smooth and combined. Stir in the remaining ingredients and mix well.

2 Press the mixture into the prepared tin and bake for about 20–25 minutes until just set. Mark into squares or bars while still hot. Leave to cool in the tin.

3 To make the topping, stir the carob and cream in a small pan over a low heat. Spread over the cookies and sprinkle the apricots on top.

Carob and Cherry Cookies

Simplicity itself to make, these little cookies are given a chocolate-like flavour by the addition of carob and are deliciously crisp and crunchy.

Makes about 20

90g/3½oz/7 tbsp unsalted (sweet) butter, at room temperature, diced

75g/3oz/scant ½ cup caster (superfine) sugar

75g/3oz/⅓ cup light muscovado (brown) sugar

1 egg

150g/5oz/1¼ cups self-raising (self-rising) flour

25g/1oz/2 tbsp carob powder

50g/2oz/¼ cup glacé (candied) cherries, quartered

50g/2oz carob bar, chopped

1 Preheat the oven to 180°C/350°F/ Gas 4. Line two large baking sheets with baking parchment. Put the unsalted butter, caster sugar, muscovado sugar and the egg in a large mixing bowl and beat well together until the mixture is smooth and creamy.

2 Add the flour, carob powder, cherries and chopped carob bar to the mixture and mix well with a wooden spoon until thoroughly combined, making sure the carob powder is completely blended in.

3 Shape the mixture into walnut-size balls and place, spaced slightly apart to allow for spreading, on the prepared baking sheets.

4 Bake for about 15 minutes. Leave on the baking sheets for 5 minutes before transferring to a wire rack to cool completely.

Variations
• *If you aren't on a diet, use unsweetened cocoa powder and a bar of chocolate instead of the carob.*
• *Use raisins instead of cherries if you like.*

Granola Bar Cookies

A gloriously dense fruity, nutty and oaty mixture, packed with goodness and delicious too, these bars are an ideal snack and perfect to pack for a school lunch.

Makes 12

175g/6oz/¾ cup unsalted (sweet)
  butter, diced
150g/5oz/⅔ cup clear honey
250g/9oz/generous 1 cup demerara
  (raw) sugar
350g/12oz/3 cups jumbo oats
5ml/1 tsp ground cinnamon
75g/3oz/¾ cup pecan nut halves
75g/3oz/generous ½ cup raisins
75g/3oz/¾ cup ready-to-eat dried
  papaya, chopped
75g/3oz/¾ cup ready-to-eat dried
  apricots, chopped
50g/2oz/scant ½ cup pumpkin seeds
50g/2oz/scant ½ cup sunflower seeds
50g/2oz/2 tbsp sesame seeds
50g/2oz/½ cup ground almonds

1 Preheat the oven to 190°C/375°F/ Gas 5. Line a 23cm/9in square cake tin (pan) with baking parchment. Put the butter and honey in a large heavy pan and heat gently until the butter has melted and the mixture is completely smooth.

2 Add the demerara sugar to the pan and heat very gently, stirring constantly, until the sugar has completely dissolved. Bring the butter mixture to the boil and continue to boil for 1–2 minutes, stirring the mixture constantly until it has formed a smooth caramel sauce.

3 Add the remaining ingredients and mix together. Transfer the mixture to the tin and press down with a spoon. Bake for 15 minutes until the edges turn brown.

4 Place in the refrigerator and chill well. Turn out of the tin, peel off the parchment and cut into bars.

Apricot and Pecan Flapjack

A tried-and-tested favourite made even more delicious by the addition of maple syrup, fruit and nuts. This is a real energy booster at any time of day – great for kids and adults alike.

Makes 10

150g/5oz/⅔ cup unsalted (sweet)
  butter, diced
150g/5oz/⅔ cup light muscovado
  (brown) sugar
30ml/2 tbsp maple syrup
200g/7oz/2 cups rolled oats
50g/2oz/½ cup pecan nuts, chopped
50g/2oz/¼ cup ready-to-eat dried
  apricots, chopped

Variations

• *You can substitute walnuts for the pecan nuts if you like, although the nutty flavour won't be so intense.*
• *Use different dried fruits instead of the apricots if you like. Let children choose their own.*

I Preheat the oven to 160°C/325°F/ Gas 3. Lightly grease an 18cm/7in square shallow baking tin (pan). Put the butter, sugar and maple syrup in a large heavy pan and heat gently until the butter has melted. Remove from the heat and stir in the oats, nuts and apricots until well combined.

2 Spread evenly in the prepared tin and, using a knife, score the mixture into ten bars. Bake for about 25–30 minutes, or until golden.

3 Remove from the oven and cut through the scored lines. Leave until completely cold before removing from the tin.

Spicy Fruit Slice

A double-layered sweet cookie in which the topping combines dried fruit, with grated carrot to keep it moist. An indulgent teatime treat.

Makes 12–16

90g/3½oz/7 tbsp vegetable margarine

75g/3oz/scant ½ cup caster
  (superfine) sugar

1 egg yolk

115g/4oz/1 cup plain (all-purpose) flour

30ml/2 tbsp self-raising (self-rising) flour

30ml/2 tbsp desiccated (dry unsweetened
  shredded) coconut

icing (confectioners') sugar, for dusting

For the topping

30ml/2 tbsp ready-to-eat
  prunes, chopped

30ml/2 tbsp sultanas (golden raisins)

50g/2oz/½ cup ready-to-eat dried
  pears, chopped

25g/1oz/¼ cup walnuts, chopped

75g/3oz/⅔ cup self-raising
  (self-rising) flour

5ml/1 tsp ground cinnamon

2.5ml/½ tsp ground ginger

175g/6oz/generous 1 cup grated carrots

1 egg, beaten

75ml/5 tbsp vegetable oil

2.5ml/½ tsp bicarbonate of soda
  (baking soda)

90g/3½oz/scant ½ cup dark muscovado
  (molasses) sugar

1 Preheat the oven to 180°C/350°F/ Gas 4. Line a 28 x 18cm/11 x 7in shallow baking tin (pan) with baking parchment. In a large mixing bowl beat together the margarine, sugar and egg yolk until smooth and creamy.

Cook's Tip

There is no need to peel the carrots before grating them. Just give them a good scrub to remove any dirt.

2 Stir in the plain flour, self-raising flour and coconut and mix together well. Press into the base of the prepared tin, using your fingers to spread the dough evenly. Bake for about 15 minutes, or until firm and light brown.

3 To make the topping, mix together all the ingredients and spread over the cooked base. Bake for about 35 minutes, or until firm. Cool completely in the tin before cutting into bars or squares. Dust with icing sugar.

Date Slice

Lemon-flavoured icing tops these scrumptious, low-fat bars, which are full of succulent fruit and crunchy seeds – the perfect mid-morning pick-me-up with a cup of decaf.

Makes 12–16

175g/6oz/¾ cup light muscovado
  (brown) sugar
175g/6oz/1 cup ready-to-eat dried
  dates, chopped
115g/4oz/1 cup self-raising
  (self-rising) flour
50g/2oz/½ cup muesli (granola)
30ml/2 tbsp sunflower seeds
15ml/1 tbsp poppy seeds
30ml/2 tbsp sultanas
  (golden raisins)
150ml/¼ pint/⅔ cup plain (natural)
  low-fat yogurt
1 egg, beaten
200g/7oz/1¾ cups icing (confectioners')
  sugar, sifted
lemon juice
15–30ml/1–2 tbsp pumpkin seeds

1 Preheat the oven to 180°C/350°F/ Gas 4. Line a 28 x 18cm/11 x 7in shallow baking tin (pan) with baking parchment. Mix together all the ingredients, except the icing sugar, lemon juice and pumpkin seeds.

2 Spread in the tin and bake for about 25 minutes until golden brown. Cool.

3 To make the topping, put the icing sugar in a bowl and stir in just enough lemon juice to make a spreading consistency.

4 Spread over the baked date mixture and sprinkle generously with pumpkin seeds. Leave to set before cutting into squares or bars.

Tropical Fruit Slice

Densely packed dried exotic fruits make the filling for these deliciously moist bars. They make a popular after-school snack for hungry kids, or pop one into their lunch box as a surprise.

Makes 12–16

175g/6oz/1½ cups plain
 (all-purpose) flour
90g/3½oz/generous ½ cup white
 vegetable fat (shortening)
60ml/4 tbsp apricot jam, sieved, or
 ready-made apricot glaze

For the filling

115g/4oz/½ cup unsalted (sweet)
 butter, softened
115g/4oz/generous ½ cup caster
 (superfine) sugar
1 egg, beaten
25g/1oz/¼ cup ground almonds
25g/1oz/2½ tbsp ground rice
300g/11oz/scant 2 cups ready-to-eat
 mixed dried tropical fruits, chopped

1 Preheat the oven to 180°C/350°F/ Gas 4. Lightly grease a 28 x 18cm/ 11 x 7in tin (pan). Put the flour and vegetable fat in a bowl and rub in with your fingers until the mixture resembles fine breadcrumbs. Add enough water to mix to a firm dough.

2 Roll out on a lightly floured surface and use to line the base of the prepared tin. Spread 30ml/ 2 tbsp of the jam or glaze over the dough.

3 To make the filling, cream together the butter and sugar until light and creamy. Beat in the egg, then stir in the almonds, rice and mixed fruits. Spread the mixture evenly in the tin.

4 Bake for about 35 minutes. Remove from the oven and brush with the remaining jam or glaze. Leave to cool completely in the tin before cutting into bars.

Cook's Tip

If you cannot find a ready-mixed packet of dried tropical fruits, make your own fruit mixture, choosing from the following: mangoes, apricots, guavas, dates, apples, pears, nectarines, peaches, figs and whatever else takes your fancy.

Ultimate Indulgence

In case all the previous recipes haven't spoilt
you for choice, here is a superb collection of
mouthwatering treats that will prove totally
irresistible – from blissful Tiramisù Cookies to
light-as-air Praline Pavlova Cookies. There is
something special to indulge everyone,
whether your tastes are for the rich and
creamy, fresh and fruity or dark and chocolatey.
There are even breakfast cookies that cook
overnight while you sleep.

Midnight Cookies

These cookies are so called because you can make them up before you go to bed and leave them to bake slowly in the switched-off oven. Hey presto – there they are in the morning, lightly crunchy on the outside and deliciously soft in the middle. A wonderfully indulgent way to start the day.

Makes 9

1 egg white
90g/3½oz/½ cup caster
    (superfine) sugar
50g/2oz/½ cup ground almonds
90g/3½oz/generous ½ cup milk
    chocolate chips
90g/3½oz/scant ½ cup glacé (candied)
    cherries, chopped
50g/2oz/⅔ cup sweetened,
    shredded coconut

1 Preheat the oven to 220°C/425°F/ Gas 7. Line a baking sheet with baking parchment. Put the egg white in a large, clean, grease-free bowl and whisk until stiff peaks form.

2 Add the caster sugar to the whisked egg white, a spoonful at a time, whisking well between each addition until the sugar is fully incorporated. The mixture should be completely smooth and glossy in appearance. Use an electric mixer for speed.

3 Fold in the almonds, chocolate chips, cherries and coconut. Place 9 spoonfuls on the baking sheet. Place in the oven, close the door then turn the oven off. Leave overnight (or at least 6 hours during the day) and don't open the door. Serve the cookies for breakfast.

Banana Cream Cookies

Bananas make for a wonderful soft texture and sweet, rich flavour. The warm banana cookies are coated in crisp sugar-frosted cornflakes and, for the ultimate indulgence, are delicious served warm drizzled with clear honey.

Makes about 24

2 eggs

250g/9oz/1¼ cups soft light
  brown sugar

5ml/1 tsp vanilla essence (extract)

100ml/3½fl oz/scant ½ cup
  sunflower oil

90g/3½oz/scant ½ cup crème fraîche

200g/7oz/1¾ cups plain
  (all-purpose) flour

200g/7oz/1¾ cups self-raising
  (self-rising) flour

50g/2oz/2½ cups frosted cornflakes

125g/4¼oz dried small bananas,
  chopped, or 2 bananas, peeled
  and chopped

icing (confectioners') sugar, sifted,
  for dredging

1 Preheat the oven to 180°C/350°F/ Gas 4. Line two or three baking sheets with baking parchment. Put the eggs and brown sugar in a large bowl and whisk together until well blended. Stir in the vanilla essence. Add the oil and crème fraîche and stir in well. Add the flour and mix well. (The mixture will be quite runny at this stage.) Cover with clear film (plastic wrap) and chill in the refrigerator for about 30 minutes.

2 Put the frosted cornflakes in a large bowl. Remove the cookie dough from the refrigerator and stir in the bananas. Using a tablespoon, drop heaps into the flakes. Lightly toss so each cookie is well coated, then remove and place on the prepared baking sheets. Flatten very slightly with your fingertips.

3 Bake for 15–20 minutes, or until risen and golden brown and crispy. Transfer the cookies to a wire rack and dredge with sifted icing sugar. Serve while still warm.

Praline Pavlova Cookies

Crisp, melt-in-the-mouth meringue with a luxurious velvety chocolate filling is topped with nutty praline – just the thing for a special tea party or simply when you feel in need of a treat.

Makes 14

2 large (US extra large)
  egg whites
large pinch of ground cinnamon
90g/3½oz/½ cup caster
  (superfine) sugar
50g/2oz/½ cup pecan nuts,
  finely chopped

For the filling

50g/2oz/¼ cup unsalted (sweet) butter,
  at room temperature, diced
100g/3½oz/scant 1 cup icing
  (confectioners') sugar, sifted
50g/2oz plain (semisweet) chocolate

For the praline

60ml/4 tbsp caster (superfine) sugar
15g/½oz/1 tbsp finely chopped
  toasted almonds

2 Place 14 spoonfuls of meringue on the prepared baking sheets, spaced well apart. Using the back of a wetted teaspoon, make a small hollow in the top of each meringue so it looks like a little nest. Bake in the oven for 45–60 minutes until dry and just beginning to colour. Remove from the oven and set aside to cool.

1 Preheat the oven to 140°C/275°F/ Gas 1. Line two baking sheets with baking parchment. Put the egg whites in a bowl and whisk until stiff. Stir the cinnamon into the sugar. Add a spoonful of sugar to the egg whites and whisk well. Continue adding the sugar, a spoonful at a time, whisking well until the mixture is thick and glossy. Stir in the chopped pecan nuts.

3 To make the filling, beat together the butter and icing sugar until light and creamy. Break the chocolate into even-size pieces and place in a heatproof bowl. Set over a pan of barely simmering water and stir occasionally until melted. Remove from the heat and leave to cool slightly. Add the chocolate to the butter mixture and stir well. Divide the filling among the meringues, putting a little in each hollow.

4 To make the praline, put the sugar in a small non-stick frying pan. Heat gently until the sugar melts to form a clear liquid. When the mixture begins to turn brown, stir in the nuts. When the mixture is a golden brown, remove from the heat and pour immediately on to a lightly oiled or non-stick baking sheet. Leave to cool completely and then break into small pieces. Sprinkle over the meringues and serve.

Cook's Tip
These cookies should be eaten immediately once they have been assembled. To make them ahead of time, store the unfilled meringues in an airtight container and place the filling in a covered container in a cool place. Make the praline on the day itself.

Variation
Use toasted hazelnuts, instead of almonds, to make the praline.

Tiramisù Cookies

These delicate cookies taste like the wonderful Italian dessert with its flavours of coffee, chocolate, rum and rich creamy custard. Serve with coffee or cups of frothy hot chocolate.

Makes 14

50g/2oz/¼ cup butter, at room
   temperature, diced
90g/3½oz/½ cup caster
   (superfine) sugar
1 egg, beaten
50g/2oz/½ cup plain (all-purpose) flour

For the filling

150g/5oz/⅔ cup mascarpone cheese
15ml/1 tbsp dark rum
2.5ml/½ tsp instant coffee powder
15ml/1 tbsp light muscovado
   (molasses) sugar

For the topping

75g/3oz white chocolate
15ml/1 tbsp milk
30ml/2 tbsp crushed chocolate flakes

1 To make the filling, put the mascarpone cheese in a bowl. Mix together the rum and coffee powder, stirring well until the coffee has dissolved. Add the rum and coffee mixture and the sugar to the cheese and mix together well. Cover with clear film (plastic wrap) and chill until required.

2 Preheat the oven to 200°C/400°F/ Gas 6. Line two or three baking sheets with baking parchment. To make the cookies, cream together the butter and sugar in a bowl until light and fluffy. Add the beaten egg and mix well. Stir in the flour and mix thoroughly again until well combined.

3 Put the mixture into a piping (pastry) bag fitted with a 1.5cm/⅝in plain nozzle and pipe 28 small blobs on to the baking sheets, spaced slightly apart. Cook for about 6–8 minutes until firm in the centre and just beginning to brown on the edges. Remove from the oven and set aside to cool.

4 When ready to assemble, spread a little of the filling on to half the cookies and place the other halves on top. Put the chocolate and milk in a heatproof bowl and melt over a pan of hot water. Take care not to overheat. When the chocolate has melted, stir vigorously to make a smooth spreadable consistency. Spread the chocolate topping evenly over the cookies, then sprinkle with crushed chocolate flakes to finish.

Chocolate and Prune Cookies

When freshly baked, these cookies have a deliciously gooey centre. As they cool down the mixture hardens slightly to form a firmer, fudge-like consistency. Try these with a glass of brandy.

Makes 18
150g/5oz/⅔ cup butter, at room
temperature, diced
150g/5oz/¾ cup caster (superfine) sugar
1 egg yolk
250g/9oz/2¼ cups self-raising
(self-rising) flour
25g/1oz/¼ cup (unsweetened)
cocoa powder
about 90g/3½oz plain (semisweet)
chocolate, coarsely chopped

For the topping
50g/2oz plain (semisweet) chocolate
9 ready-to-eat prunes, halved

1 Preheat the oven to 190°C/375°F/ Gas 5. Line two baking sheets with baking parchment. Cream the butter and sugar together until light and creamy. Beat in the egg yolk. Sift over the flour and cocoa powder and stir in to make a firm yet soft dough.

2 Roll out about a third of the dough on baking parchment. Using a 5cm/2in round biscuit (cookie) cutter, stamp out 18 rounds and place them on the baking sheets.

3 Sprinkle the chopped chocolate in the centre of each cookie.

4 Roll out the remaining dough in the same way as before and, using a 7.5cm/3in round biscuit cutter, stamp out 18 "lids". Carefully lay the lids over the cookie bases and press the edges well together to seal. Don't worry if the lids crack slightly when you do this.

5 Bake for about 10 minutes until the cookies have spread a little and are just firm to a light touch. Leave them on the baking sheets for about 5 minutes to firm up slightly, then, using a palette knife (metal spatula), transfer to a wire rack to cool completely.

6 For the topping, melt the chocolate in a heatproof bowl set over a pan of hot water. Dip the cut side of the prunes in the chocolate then place one on top of each cookie. Spoon any remaining chocolate over the prunes.

Ice Cream Sandwich Cookies

These are great when you get those midnight munchies – either keep the cookies in an airtight container and sandwich together each time with the softened ice cream of your choice or make the sandwiches complete with ice cream and coating and freeze until required.

Makes 12
115g/4oz/½ cup unsalted (sweet) butter,
*   at room temperature, diced*
115g/4oz/generous ½ cup caster
*   (superfine) sugar*
1 egg, beaten
200g/7oz/1¾ cups plain
*   (all-purpose) flour*
25g/1oz/¼ cup (unsweetened)
*   cocoa powder, sieved*
ice cream, to fill
toasted nuts, biscuit (cookie) crumbs,
*   chocolate flakes or demerara (raw)*
*   sugar, to coat*

1 Preheat the oven to 180°C/350°F/ Gas 4. Cream the butter and sugar together until light and fluffy, then beat in the egg. Stir in the flour and cocoa powder to make a firm dough.

3 To make the ice cream cookies, spread 2 good spoonfuls of softened ice cream on a cookie and press a second on top. Squeeze so the filling reaches the edges.

4 Put your chosen coating on a plate and roll the cookies in it to coat the sides. Either eat straight away or wrap individually in foil and freeze. The cookies may be kept for up to 2 weeks in the freezer.

Cook's Tip
For super deluxe cookies, half-dip the ice cream cookies in melted chocolate. Shake off the excess, place on a sheet of baking parchment and freeze at once. When the chocolate has set, either eat or wrap in foil and freeze for later.

2 Roll the dough out to a thickness of 6mm/¼in on baking parchment. Using a 7.5cm/3in plain round biscuit (cookie) cutter, stamp out 24 rounds and place on the prepared baking sheets. Alternatively cut into squares or rectangles of equal size. Bake the cookies for about 15 minutes. Set aside on the baking sheets to cool.

Nut Bar Cookies

If you love chocolate, condensed milk, nuts and crumb crust then these are the cookies for you. It's fortunate that they are incredibly easy to make because they are even easier to eat and are sure to become firm favourites with all the family. Children enjoy helping to make them.

Makes 16–18

250g/9oz digestive biscuits
 (graham crackers)
115g/4oz/½ cup butter, melted
150g/5oz/scant 1 cup milk
 chocolate chips
200g/7oz mixed whole nuts, such as
 pecan nuts, hazelnuts, brazil nuts,
 walnuts and almonds
200ml/7fl oz/scant 1 cup can sweetened
 condensed milk

Cook's Tip

If you prefer, use a shallow 20cm/8in cake tin (pan) instead, and cut the cookies into squares.

1 Preheat the oven to 180°C/350°F/ Gas 4. Crush the biscuits in a polythene bag with a rolling pin.

2 Put the biscuit crumbs in a bowl and stir in the melted butter. Mix well. Press the mixture evenly into the base of a 10 x 36cm/4 x 14in cake tin (pan).

3 Sprinkle the chocolate chips over the biscuit base. Arrange the nuts on top and pour the condensed milk over the top evenly.

4 Bake for 25 minutes, or until bubbling and golden. Cool in the tin, loosen from the sides, then cool completely and slice into thin bars.

Apple Crumble and Custard Slice

These luscious apple slices are easy to make using ready-made sweet pastry and custard.
Just think, all the ingredients of one of the world's most popular desserts – in a cookie.

Makes 16

350g/12oz ready-made sweet pastry
1 large cooking apple, about 250g/9oz
30ml/2 tbsp caster (superfine) sugar
60ml/4 tbsp ready-made thick custard

For the crumble topping

115g/4oz/1 cup plain (all-purpose) flour
2.5ml/½ tsp ground cinnamon
60ml/4 tbsp granulated sugar
90g/3½oz/7 tbsp unsalted (sweet)
* butter, melted*

1 Preheat the oven to 190°C/375°F/
Gas 5. Roll out the pastry and use
to line the base of a 28 x 18cm/
11 x 7in shallow cake tin (pan).
Prick the pastry with a fork, line
with foil and baking beans and bake
blind for about 10–15 minutes.
Remove the foil and baking beans
and return the pastry to the oven
for a further 5 minutes until cooked
and golden brown.

2 Meanwhile, peel, core and chop
the apple evenly. Place in a pan
with the sugar. Heat gently until the
sugar dissolves, then cover with a lid
and cook gently for 5–7 minutes
until a thick purée is formed. Beat
with a wooden spoon and set
aside to cool.

3 Mix the cold apple with the
custard. Spread over the pastry.

4 To make the crumble topping, put
the flour, cinnamon and sugar into a
bowl and pour over the melted
butter. Stir thoroughly until the
mixture forms small clumps. Sprinkle
the crumble over the filling.

5 Return to the oven and bake for
about 10–15 minutes until the
crumble topping is cooked and a
golden brown. Leave to cool in the
tin, then slice into bars to serve.

Creamy Fig and Peach Squares

A sweet cream cheese and dried fruit filling with a hint of mint makes these cookies really special. They are ideal for quietening hunger pangs after school or work.

Makes 24

350g/12oz/3 cups plain (all-purpose) flour
200g/7oz/scant 1 cup unsalted
   (sweet) butter, diced
1 egg, beaten
caster (superfine) sugar,
   for sprinkling

For the filling

500g/1¼lb/2½ cups ricotta cheese
115g/4oz/generous ½ cup
   caster (superfine) sugar
5ml/1 tsp finely chopped fresh mint
50g/2oz/⅓ cup ready-to-eat dried
   figs, chopped
50g/2oz/⅓ cup ready-to-eat dried
   peaches, chopped

1 Preheat the oven to 190°C/375°F/ Gas 5. And then lightly grease a 33 x 23cm/13 x 9in Swiss roll tin (jelly roll pan) or shallow cake tin (pan). Put the flour and butter into a bowl. Rub in the butter until the mixture resembles fine breadcrumbs. Add the egg and enough water to mix to a firm but not sticky dough.

2 Divide the pastry into two and roll out one piece to fit the base of the prepared tin. Place in the tin and trim.

3 To make the filling, put all the ingredients in a bowl and mix together. Spread over the pastry base. Roll out the remaining pastry and place on top of the filling. Prick lightly all over with a fork then sprinkle with caster sugar.

4 Bake for about 30 minutes until light golden brown. Remove from the oven and sprinkle more caster sugar thickly over the top. Cool and cut into slices to serve.

Dessert Cookies

Mousses, sorbets, ice creams and fresh fruit salads are among the many desserts complemented by delicate, elegant or richly flavoured cookies – and, of course, there is nothing so delicious as special little nibbles served with coffee and liqueurs. The recipes in this chapter will be an inspiration for those who love to entertain, as they provide that professional finishing touch that turns a good meal into a truly memorable occasion.

Rosemary-scented Citrus Tuiles

These delicious crisp cookies are flavoured with tangy orange and lemon rind, and made beautifully fragrant with fresh rosemary – an unusual but winning combination.

Makes 18–20

50g/2oz/¼ cup unsalted (sweet)
   butter, diced
2 egg whites
115g/4oz/generous ½ cup caster
   (superfine) sugar
finely grated rind of ½ lemon
finely grated rind of ½ orange
10ml/2 tsp finely chopped fresh rosemary
50g/2oz/½ cup plain (all-purpose) flour

1 Preheat the oven to 190°C/375°F/ Gas 5. Line a baking sheet with baking parchment. Melt the butter in a pan over a low heat. Leave to cool. Whisk the egg whites until stiff, then gradually whisk in the sugar.

2 Fold in the lemon and orange rinds, rosemary and flour and then the melted butter. Place 2 large tablespoonfuls of mixture on the baking sheet. Spread each to a thin disc about 9cm/3½in in diameter. Bake for 5–6 minutes until golden.

3 Remove from the oven and lift the tuiles using a palette knife (metal spatula) and drape over a rolling pin. Transfer to a wire rack when set in a curved shape. Continue baking the rest of the mixture in the same way.

Ginger Glass Cookies

As thin, delicate and elegant as fine glass, these ginger cookies are ideal served with creamy desserts, syllabubs, sorbets and luxury ice creams.

Makes about 18

50g/2oz/¼ cup unsalted (sweet) butter, diced
40g/1½oz/3 tbsp liquid glucose (clear corn syrup)
90g/3½oz/½ cup caster (superfine) sugar
40g/1½oz/⅓ cup plain (all-purpose) flour
5ml/1 tsp ground ginger

1 Put the butter and liquid glucose in a heatproof bowl set over a pan of gently simmering water. Stir together until melted. Set aside.

Cook's Tip
Use unlipped baking sheets so you can roll the cookies thinly.

2 Put the sugar in a bowl and sift over the flour and ginger. Stir into the butter mixture, then beat well until combined. Cover with clear film (plastic wrap) and chill for about 25 minutes, until firm. Meanwhile, preheat the oven to 180°C/350°F/ Gas 4 and line two or three baking sheets with baking parchment.

3 Roll teaspoonfuls of the cookie mixture into balls between your hands and place them, spaced well apart to allow room for spreading, on the prepared baking sheets.

4 Place a second piece of baking parchment on top and roll the cookies as thinly as possible. Peel off the top sheet. Then stamp each cookie with a 7.5 or 9cm/3 or 3½in plain round cutter.

5 Bake for 5–6 minutes, or until golden. Leave for a few seconds on the baking sheets to firm up slightly, then either leave flat or curl over in half. Leave to cool completely.

Lace Cookies

Very pretty, delicate and crisp, these lacy cookies are ideal for serving with elegant creamy or iced desserts at the end of a dinner party. Don't be tempted to bake more than four on a sheet.

Makes about 14

75g/3oz/6 tbsp butter, diced
75g/3oz/¾ cup rolled oats
115g/4oz/generous ½ cup golden caster
  (superfine) sugar
1 egg, beaten
10ml/2 tsp plain (all-purpose)
  flour
5ml/1 tsp baking powder
2.5ml/½ tsp mixed (apple pie)
  spice

1 Preheat the oven to 180°C/350°F/ Gas 4. Line three or four baking sheets with baking parchment. Put the butter in a pan and set over a low heat until just melted. Remove the pan from the heat.

2 Stir the rolled oats into the melted butter. Add the remaining ingredients and mix well.

3 Place only 3 or 4 heaped teaspoonfuls of the mixture, spaced well apart, on each of the lined baking sheets.

4 Bake for about 5–7 minutes, or until a deepish golden brown all over. Leave the cookies on the baking sheets for a few minutes. Carefully cut the parchment so you can lift each cookie singly. Invert on to a wire rack and carefully remove the parchment. Leave to cool.

Florentine Bites

Very sweet and rich, these little mouthfuls are great with after-dinner coffee and liqueurs, and would also make an ideal and special gift to offer to a dinner party host.

Makes 36

200g/7oz good quality plain (semisweet)
  chocolate (minimum 70 per cent
  cocoa solids)
50g/2oz/2½ cups cornflakes
50g/2oz/scant ½ cup sultanas
  (golden raisins)
115g/4oz/1 cup toasted flaked
  (sliced) almonds
115g/4oz/½ cup glacé (candied)
  cherries, halved
50g/2oz/⅓ cup cut mixed (candied) peel
200ml/7fl oz/scant 1 cup can sweetened
  condensed milk

1 Preheat the oven to 180°C/350°F/ Gas 4. Line the base of a shallow 20cm/8in cake tin (pan) with baking parchment. Lightly grease the sides. Melt the chocolate in a heatproof bowl set over a pan of hot water. Spread evenly over the base of the tin. Put in the refrigerator to set.

2 Meanwhile, put the cornflakes, sultanas, almonds, cherries and mixed peel in a large bowl. Pour over the condensed milk and toss the mixture gently, using a fork.

3 Spread the mixture evenly over the chocolate base and bake for 12–15 minutes until golden brown. Cool in the tin, then chill for 20 minutes. Cut into tiny squares.

Almond and Vanilla Cookies with Praline Coating

These short-textured almond cookies, filled with vanilla cream and coated in praline, are just the thing to have with an espresso – a sweet *bonne bouche* to counter the strong coffee.

Makes 17–18
150g/5oz/1¼ cups plain
   (all-purpose) flour
75g/3oz/¾ cup ground almonds
75g/3oz/6 tbsp unsalted (sweet) butter,
   at room temperature, diced
1 egg yolk
5ml/1 tsp vanilla essence (extract)
icing (confectioners') sugar, sifted,
   for dusting

For the praline
25g/1oz/¼ cup whole blanched almonds
50g/2oz/¼ cup caster (superfine) sugar

For the filling
150g/5oz/1¼ cups icing (confectioners')
   sugar, sifted
75g/3oz/6 tbsp unsalted (sweet) butter,
   at room temperature, diced
5ml/1 tsp vanilla essence (extract)

1 First make the praline. Lightly oil a baking sheet and place the almonds on it, fairly close together. Melt the sugar in a small non-stick pan over a very low heat. Continue heating until it turns dark golden brown and pour immediately over the almonds. Set aside to cool. Crush the praline finely in a food processor.

2 Preheat the oven to 160°C/325°F/ Gas 3. Line three baking sheets with baking parchment.

3 Put the flour, ground almonds and butter in a bowl. Rub together until the mixture starts to cling together. Add the egg and vanilla and work together using your hands to make a soft but not sticky dough. Roll out to a thickness of about 5mm/¼in on baking parchment. Using a 5cm/2in round biscuit (cookie) cutter, stamp out rounds and place them on the prepared baking sheets.

4 Bake the cookies for about 15–20 minutes, or until light golden brown. Leave on the baking sheets for 5 minutes to firm up slightly, then transfer to a wire rack to cool.

5 To make the filling, beat together the icing sugar, butter and vanilla until light and creamy. Use this mixture to sandwich the cookies in pairs. Be generous with the filling, spreading right to the edges. Press the cookies gently so the filling oozes out of the sides and, using your finger, smooth around the sides of the cookie.

6 Put the praline on a plate and roll the edges of each cookie in the praline until thickly coated. Dust the tops of the cookies with icing sugar.

Cook's Tip
These cookies should be made on the day of serving or the filling will cause them to become soggy and unpleasant.

Chocolate and Pistachio Wedges

These cookies are rich and grainy textured, with a bitter chocolate flavour. They go extremely well with vanilla ice cream and are especially delicious with bananas and custard.

Makes 16

200g/7oz/scant 1 cup unsalted (sweet) butter, at room temperature, diced
90g/3½oz/½ cup golden caster (superfine) sugar
250g/9oz/2¼ cups plain (all-purpose) flour
50g/2oz/½ cup (unsweetened) cocoa powder
25g/1oz/¼ cup shelled pistachio nuts, finely chopped
(unsweetened) cocoa powder, for dusting

1 Preheat the oven to 180°C/350°F/ Gas 4 and line a shallow 23cm/9in round sandwich tin (pan) with baking parchment.

2 Beat the butter and sugar until light and creamy. Sift the flour and cocoa powder, then add the flour mixture to the butter and work in with your hands until the mixture is smooth. Knead until soft and pliable then press into the prepared tin.

3 Using the back of a tablespoon, spread the mixture evenly in the tin. Sprinkle the pistachio nuts over the top and press in gently. Prick with a fork, then mark into 16 segments using a round-bladed knife.

4 Bake for about 15–20 minutes. Do not allow to brown at all or the cookies will taste bitter.

5 Remove the tin from the oven and dust the cookies with cocoa powder. Cut through the marked sections with a round-bladed knife and leave to cool completely before removing from the tin.

Dark Chocolate Fingers

With their understated elegance and distinctly grown-up flavour, these deliciously decadent chocolate fingers are ideal for serving with after-dinner coffee and liqueurs.

Makes about 26

115g/4oz/1 cup plain (all-purpose) flour
2.5ml/½ tsp baking powder
30ml/2 tbsp (unsweetened)
  cocoa powder
50g/2oz/¼ cup unsalted (sweet)
  butter, softened
50g/2oz/¼ cup caster (superfine) sugar
20ml/4 tsp golden (light corn) syrup
150g/5oz dark (bittersweet) chocolate
chocolate-flavour mini flakes,
  for sprinkling

1 Preheat the oven to 160°C/325°F/ Gas 3. Line two baking sheets with baking parchment. Put the flour, baking powder, cocoa powder, butter, sugar and syrup in a large mixing bowl.

2 Work the ingredients together with your hands to combine and form into a dough.

3 Roll the dough out between sheets of baking parchment to an 18 x 24cm/7 x 9½in rectangle. Remove the top sheet. Cut in half lengthways, then into bars 2cm/¾in wide. Place on the baking sheets.

4 Bake for about 15 minutes, taking care not to allow the bars to brown or they will taste bitter. Transfer to a wire rack to cool.

5 Melt the chocolate in a heatproof bowl set over a pan of hot water. Half-dip the cookies, place on baking parchment, sprinkle with chocolate flakes, then leave to set.

Mini Fudge Bites

These cute little cookies have the flavour of butterscotch and fudge and are topped with chopped pecan nuts for a delicious crunch – just the right size for a special little treat.

Makes 30

200g/7oz/1¾ cups self-raising (self-rising) flour
115g/4oz/½ cup butter, at room temperature, diced
115g/4oz/generous ½ cup dark muscovado (molasses) sugar
75g/3oz vanilla cream fudge, diced
1 egg, beaten
25g/1oz/¼ cup pecan nut halves, sliced widthways

1 Preheat the oven to 190°C/375°F/ Gas 5. Line two or three baking sheets with baking parchment. Put the flour in a bowl and rub in the butter until the mixture resembles fine breadcrumbs.

2 Add the muscovado sugar and diced vanilla cream fudge to the flour mixture and stir well until combined. Add the beaten egg and mix in well. Bring the dough together with your hands, then knead gently on a lightly floured surface. It will be soft yet firm.

3 Roll the dough into two cylinders, 23cm/9in long. Cut into 1cm/½in slices and place on the baking sheets. Sprinkle over the pecan nuts and press in lightly. Bake for about 12 minutes until browned at the edges. Transfer to a wire rack to cool.

Chocolate Truffle Cookies

Deeply decadent, chocolatey truffle cookies are given a wicked twist by the addition of cherry brandy – the perfect way to end dinner.

Makes 18

50g/2oz/½ cup plain
  (all-purpose) flour
25g/1oz/¼ cup (unsweetened)
  cocoa powder
2.5ml/½ tsp baking powder
90g/3½oz/½ cup caster
  (superfine) sugar
25g/1oz/2 tbsp butter, diced
1 egg, beaten
5ml/1 tsp cherry brandy or fresh
  orange juice
50g/2oz/½ cup icing
  (confectioners') sugar

1 Preheat the oven to 200°C/400°F/ Gas 6. Line two baking sheets with baking parchment.

2 Sift the flour, cocoa and baking powder into a bowl and stir in the sugar. Rub in the butter until the mixture resembles breadcrumbs. Mix together the beaten egg and cherry brandy or orange juice and stir into the flour mixture. Cover with clear film (plastic wrap) and chill in the refrigerator for 30 minutes.

3 Put the icing sugar into a bowl. Shape walnut-size pieces of dough roughly into a ball and drop into the icing sugar. Toss until thickly coated then place on the baking sheets.

4 Bake for about 10 minutes, or until just set. Transfer to a wire rack to cool completely.

Brownies and Bars

Cookies with attitude, brownies and bars make filling snacks, lunchtime treats, perfect picnic fare and a marvellous morale and energy boost at any time of day. There are probably more variations on the basic brownie than on any other cookie in the world and when you try some of the recipes here, you will understand why. As for bars and slices, the sky's the limit – crisp and nutty, chewy and succulent, sweet and fruity. You choose.

Chocolate Cheesecake Brownies

A very dense chocolate brownie mixture is swirled with creamy cheese to give a marbled effect. Cut into tiny squares for little mouthfuls of absolute heaven.

Makes 16

For the cheesecake mixture

1 egg
225g/8oz/1 cup full-fat
   cream cheese
50g/2oz/¼ cup caster
   (superfine) sugar
5ml/1 tsp vanilla essence (extract)

For the brownie mixture

115g/4oz dark (bittersweet)
   chocolate (minimum 70 per cent
   cocoa solids)
115g/4oz/½ cup unsalted
   (sweet) butter
150g/5oz/¾ cup light muscovado
   (brown) sugar
2 eggs, beaten
50g/2oz/½ cup plain
   (all-purpose) flour

1 Preheat the oven to 160°C/ 325°F/Gas 3. Line the base and sides of a 20cm/8in cake tin (pan) with baking parchment.

2 To make the cheesecake mixture, beat the egg in a mixing bowl, then add the cream cheese, caster sugar and vanilla essence. Beat together until smooth and creamy.

3 To make the brownie mixture, melt the chocolate and butter together in the microwave or in a heatproof bowl set over a pan of gently simmering water. When the mixture is melted, remove from the heat, stir well, then add the sugar. Add the eggs, a little at a time, and beat well. Gently stir in the flour.

4 Spread two-thirds of the brownie mixture over the base of the tin. Spread the cheesecake mixture on top, then spoon on the remaining brownie mixture in heaps. Using a skewer, swirl the mixtures together.

5 Bake for 30–35 minutes, or until just set in the centre. Leave to cool in the tin, then cut into squares.

Butterscotch Brownies

These gorgeous treats are made with brown sugar, white chocolate chips and walnuts. Who could possibly have the will power to resist? You might want to make two batches at a time.

Makes 12

450g/1lb white chocolate chips
75g/3oz/6 tbsp unsalted (sweet) butter
3 eggs
*175g/6oz/¾ cup light muscovado
  (brown) sugar*
*175g/6oz/1½ cups self-raising
  (self-rising) flour*
175g/6oz/1½ cups walnuts, chopped
5ml/1 tsp vanilla essence (extract)

1 Preheat the oven to 190°C/ 375°F/Gas 5. Line the base of a 28 x 18cm/11 x 7in shallow tin (pan) with baking parchment. Lightly grease the sides. Melt 90g/3½oz of the chocolate chips with the butter in a bowl set over a pan of hot water. Leave to cool slightly.

2 Put the eggs and light muscovado sugar into a large bowl and whisk well, then whisk in the melted chocolate mixture.

3 Sift in the flour into the bowl and gently fold in along with the chopped walnuts, vanilla essence and the remaining chocolate chips. Be careful not to overmix.

4 Spread the mixture out in the prepared tin and bake for about 30 minutes, or until risen and golden brown. The centre should be firm to the touch but will be slightly soft until it cools down.

5 Leave to cool in the tin, then cut into twelve bars when the brownie is completely cool.

Luscious Lemon Bars

A crisp cookie base is covered with a tangy lemon topping. The bars make a delightful addition to the tea table on a warm summer's day in the garden.

Makes 12

150g/5oz/1¼ cups plain
  (all-purpose) flour
90g/3½oz/7 tbsp unsalted (sweet) butter,
  chilled and diced
50g/2oz/½ cup icing (confectioners')
  sugar, sifted

For the topping

2 eggs
175g/6oz/scant 1 cup caster
  (superfine) sugar
finely grated rind and juice of
  1 large lemon
15ml/1 tbsp plain (all-purpose) flour
2.5ml/½ tsp bicarbonate of soda
  (baking soda)
icing (confectioners') sugar, for dusting

3 To make the topping, whisk the eggs in a bowl until frothy. Add the caster sugar, a little at a time, whisking well between each addition. Whisk in the lemon rind and juice, flour and soda. Pour over the cookie base. Bake for 20–25 minutes, until set and golden.

4 Leave to cool slightly. Cut into twelve bars and dust lightly with icing sugar. Leave to cool completely.

1 Preheat the oven to 180°C/350°F/ Gas 4. Line the base of a 20cm/8in square shallow cake tin (pan) with baking parchment and lightly grease the sides of the tin.

2 Process the flour, butter and icing sugar in a food processor until the mixture comes together as a firm dough. Press evenly into the base of the tin and spread smoothly using the back of a tablespoon. Bake for 12–15 minutes until lightly golden. Cool in the tin.

Sticky Marmalade Squares

These baked treats have a plain lower layer supporting a scrumptious nutty upper layer flavoured with orange and chunky marmalade. Cut into squares or bars – whichever you prefer.

Makes 24

350g/12oz/3 cups plain
  (all-purpose) flour
200g/7oz/scant 1 cup unsalted (sweet)
  butter, diced
150g/5oz/⅔ cup light muscovado
  (molasses) sugar
2.5ml/½ tsp bicarbonate of soda
  (baking soda)
1 egg, beaten
120ml/4fl oz/½ cup single
  (light) cream
50g/2oz/½ cup pecan nuts, chopped
50g/2oz/⅓ cup mixed (candied) peel
90ml/6 tbsp chunky marmalade
15–30ml/1–2 tbsp orange juice

1 Preheat the oven to 190°C/ 375°F/Gas 5. Line the base of a 28 x 18cm/11 x 7in tin (pan) with baking parchment.

2 Put the flour in a bowl and rub in the butter. Stir in the sugar and then spread half the mixture over the base of the prepared tin. Press down firmly. Bake for 10–15 minutes until lightly browned. Leave to cool.

3 To make the filling, put the remaining flour mixture into a bowl. Stir in the soda. Mix in the egg and cream, pecan nuts, peel and half the marmalade.

4 Pour the mixture over the cooled base, return to the oven and bake for 20–25 minutes, or until the filling is just firm and golden brown.

5 Put the remaining marmalade into a small pan and heat gently. Add just enough orange juice to make a spreadable glaze. Brush the glaze over the baked cookie mixture while it is still warm. Leave to cool before cutting into bars or squares.

Variation
These bars would be just as delicious made with lemon, lime, grapefruit or mixed fruit marmalade instead of orange. However, do not substitute a sharper juice, such as lemon, for the orange juice as this would spoil the flavour.

Walnut and Honey Bars

A sweet, custard-like filling brimming with nuts sits on a crisp pastry base. These scrumptious bars are pure heaven to bite into.

Makes 12–14

175g/6oz/1½ cups plain
   (all-purpose) flour
30ml/2 tbsp icing (confectioners')
   sugar, sifted
115g/4oz/½ cup unsalted (sweet)
   butter, diced

For the filling

300g/11oz/scant 3 cups walnut halves
2 eggs, beaten
50g/2oz/¼ cup unsalted (sweet)
   butter, melted
50g/2oz/¼ cup light muscovado
   (brown) sugar
90ml/6 tbsp dark clear honey
30ml/2 tbsp single (light) cream

1 Preheat the oven to 190°C/375°F/
Gas 5. Lightly grease a 28 x 18cm/
11 x 7in shallow tin (pan).

2 Put the flour, icing sugar and
butter in a food processor
and process until the mixture forms
crumbs. Using the pulse button, add
15–30ml/1–2 tbsp water – enough
to make a firm dough.

3 Roll the dough out on baking
parchment and line the base and
sides of the tin. Trim and fold the
top edge inwards.

4 Prick the base, line with foil and
baking beans and bake blind for
10 minutes. Remove the foil and
beans. Return the base to the oven
for about 5 minutes, until cooked
but not browned. Reduce the
temperature to 180°C/350°F/Gas 4.

5 For the filling, sprinkle the walnuts
over the base. Whisk the remaining
ingredients together. Pour over the
walnuts and bake for 25 minutes.

Mincemeat Wedges

The flour used in these wedge-shaped cookies gives a nutty flavour that combines well with the mincemeat. These are great for winter tea parties around a blazing fire.

Makes 12

225g/8oz/2 cups self-raising (self-rising)
   wholemeal (whole-wheat) flour
75g/3oz/6 tbsp unsalted (sweet)
   butter, diced
75g/3oz/⅓ cup demerara (raw) sugar
1 egg, beaten
115g/4oz/⅓ cup good-quality mincemeat
about 60ml/4 tbsp milk
crushed brown or white café (sugar)
   cubes or a mixture, for sprinkling

Cook's Tip
If you can't find self-raising (self-rising) flour, add 10ml/2 tsp baking powder to the plain wholemeal (whole-wheat) flour.

I Preheat the oven to 200°C/400°F/ Gas 6. Line the base of a 20cm/8in round sandwich tin (layer pan) and lightly grease the sides. Put the flour in a bowl, add the diced butter and rub in with your fingertips just until the mixture resembles coarse breadcrumbs.

2 Stir in the demerara sugar, egg and mincemeat. Add enough milk to mix to a soft dough. Spread evenly in the prepared tin and sprinkle generously with the crushed sugar. Bake for about 20 minutes until firm and golden. Cool in the tin, then cut into wedges to serve.

Almond, Orange and Carrot Bars

An out-of-this-world cookie version of the ever-popular carrot cake, these flavoursome, moist bars are best eaten fresh or stored in the refrigerator after making.

Makes 16

75g/3oz/6 tbsp unsalted (sweet)
 butter, softened
50g/2oz/¼ cup caster (superfine) sugar
150g/5oz/1¼ cups plain
 (all-purpose) flour
finely grated rind of 1 orange

For the filling

90g/3½oz/7 tbsp unsalted (sweet)
 butter, diced
75g/3oz/scant ½ cup caster
 (superfine) sugar
2 eggs
2.5ml/½ tsp almond essence (extract)
175g/6oz/1½ cups ground almonds
1 cooked carrot, coarsely grated

For the topping

175g/6oz/¾ cup cream cheese
30–45ml/2–3 tbsp chopped walnuts

1 Preheat the oven to 190°C/375°F/ Gas 5. Lightly grease a 28 x 18cm/ 11 x 7in shallow baking tin (pan). Put the butter, caster sugar, flour and orange rind into a bowl and rub together until the mixture resembles coarse breadcrumbs. Add water, a teaspoon at a time, to mix to a firm but not sticky dough. Roll out on a lightly floured surface and use to line the base of the tin.

2 To make the filling, cream the butter and sugar together. Beat in the eggs and almond essence. Stir in the ground almonds and the grated carrot. Spread the mixture over the dough base and bake for about 25 minutes until firm in the centre and golden brown. Leave to cool in the tin.

3 To make the topping, beat the cream cheese until smooth and spread it over the cooled, cooked filling. Swirl with a small palette knife (metal spatula) and sprinkle with the chopped walnuts. Cut into bars with a sharp knife.

Hazelnut and Raspberry Bars

The hazelnuts are ground and used to make a superb sweet pastry which is then baked with a layer of raspberry jam in the middle and sprinkled with flaked almonds.

Makes 30

250g/9oz/2¼ cups hazelnuts
300g/10oz/2½ cups plain
  (all-purpose) flour
5ml/1 tsp mixed (apple pie) spice
2.5ml/½ tsp ground cinnamon
150g/5oz/1¼ cups golden icing
  (confectioners') sugar
15ml/1 tbsp grated lemon rind
300g/10oz/1¼ cups unsalted (sweet)
  butter, softened
3 egg yolks
350g/12oz/1¼ cups seedless
  raspberry jam

For the topping

1 egg, beaten
15ml/1 tbsp clear honey
50g/2oz/½ cup flaked (sliced) almonds

1 Grind the hazelnuts in a food processor and then put in a bowl. Sift in the flour, spices and icing sugar. Add the lemon rind and mix well, then add the butter and the egg yolks and, using your hands, knead until a smooth dough is formed. Wrap in clear film (plastic wrap) and chill for 30 minutes. Meanwhile, preheat the oven to 200°C/400°F/Gas 6 and lightly grease a 33 x 23cm/13 x 9in Swiss roll tin (jelly roll pan).

2 Roll out half the dough to fit the base of the prepared tin and place in the tin. Spread the jam all over the dough base. Roll out the remaining dough and place on top of the jam.

3 To make the topping, beat the egg and honey together and brush over the dough. Sprinkle the almonds evenly over the top.

4 Bake for 10 minutes, then lower the oven temperature to 180°C/350°F/Gas 4 and bake for another 20–30 minutes until golden brown. Cool then cut into bars.

Cook's Tip

Don't use ready-ground hazelnuts for these bars as they lose their flavour very quickly.

Cookies for Special Diets

Food intolerances, allergies and health problems need not deprive you of the pleasures of baking and eating home-made cookies. You will be amazed by the range of low-fat, dairy-free, reduced-sugar or gluten-free sweet treats you can make – and what's more, they're so scrumptious, the whole family will be clamouring for them. Whether layered slices or fabulous brownies, the cookies in this chapter are special in every way.

Very Low-fat Brownies

If you ever need proof that you can still enjoy sweet treats even when you are on a low-fat diet, here it is. These brownies are not just tasty, but also very quick and easy to make.

Makes 16

100g/3½oz/scant 1 cup plain
   (all-purpose) flour
2.5ml/½ tsp baking powder
45ml/3 tbsp (unsweetened) cocoa
   powder
200g/7oz/1 cup caster (superfine) sugar
100ml/3½fl oz/scant ½ cup natural
   (plain) low-fat yogurt
2 eggs, beaten
5ml/1 tsp vanilla essence (extract)
25ml/1½ tbsp vegetable oil

1 Preheat the oven to 180°C/350°F/ Gas 4. Line a 20cm/8in square cake tin (pan) with baking parchment.

2 Sift the flour, baking powder and cocoa powder into a bowl. Stir in the caster sugar, then beat in the yogurt, eggs, vanilla and vegetable oil until thoroughly combined. Put the mixture into the prepared tin.

3 Bake for about 25 minutes until just firm to the touch. Leave in the tin until cooled completely.

4 Using a sharp knife, cut into 16 squares, then remove from the tin using a spatula.

Carob Chip Shorties

Perfect for anyone on a gluten-free or cow's-milk-free diet, these lovely cookies are best eaten freshly made, preferably while still slightly warm from the oven.

Makes 12

175g/6oz/1½ cups gluten-free flour
25g/1oz/2 tbsp soft light brown sugar
75g/3oz/6 tbsp vegetable margarine
50g/2oz/⅓ cup carob chips
15–25ml/1–1½ tbsp clear honey, warmed
demerara (raw) or caster (superfine) sugar, for sprinkling

I Preheat the oven to 160°C/325°F/Gas 3. Line two baking sheets with baking parchment.

Cook's Tip

Gluten-free flour can be bought at most health-food stores.

2 Put the flour and brown sugar in a mixing bowl and rub in the margarine. Add the carob chips, then stir in just enough honey to bring the mixture together but not make it sticky. Roll the dough out between two sheets of baking parchment to about 8mm/⅓in.

3 Stamp out rounds using a plain 5cm/2in round biscuit (cookie) cutter. Place on the baking sheets. Prick each cookie once with a fork and sprinkle with sugar.

4 Bake for about 15–20 minutes, or until firm. Cool on a wire rack.

Cashew Nut Button Cookies

These light little cookies, flavoured with ground cashew nuts, are coated in toasted hazelnuts. They are suitable for people on gluten-free and cow's-milk-free diets.

Makes about 20

1 egg white
25g/1oz/2 tbsp caster (superfine) sugar
150g/5oz/1¼ cups unroasted cashew nuts, ground
50g/2oz/⅓ cup dates, finely chopped
5ml/1 tsp finely grated orange rind
30ml/2 tbsp pure maple or maple-flavoured syrup
90g/3½oz/scant 1 cup toasted hazelnuts, chopped

1 Preheat the oven to 190°C/375°F/ Gas 5. Line two baking sheets with baking parchment.

2 In a bowl, whisk the egg white until stiff. Whisk in the sugar. Stir in the cashews, dates, orange rind and syrup. Mix well. Put the chopped hazelnuts in a small bowl.

3 Drop small spoonfuls of the cookie mixture into the hazelnuts and toss until well coated.

4 Place on the prepared baking sheets and bake for about 10 minutes until lightly browned. Leave to cool on the baking sheets.

Fruit and Millet Treacle Cookies

These little cookies are quick to make, and will no doubt disappear just as quickly when they come out of the oven. They are gluten- and cow's milk-free.

Makes about 25–30

90g/3½oz/7 tbsp vegetable
*   margarine*
150g/5oz/⅔ cup light muscovado
*   (brown) sugar*
30ml/2 tbsp black treacle (molasses)
1 egg
150g/5oz/1¼ cups gluten-free flour
50g/2oz/½ cup millet flakes
50g/2oz/½ cup almonds, chopped
200g/7oz/generous 1 cup luxury
*   mixed dried fruit*

Cook's Tip

Make sure that you use millet flakes for these cookies rather than millet grains. The grains will swell too much during cooking and spoil the cookies.

1 Preheat the oven to 190°C/375°F/ Gas 5. Line two large baking sheets with baking parchment.

2 Put the margarine, muscovado sugar, treacle and egg in a large bowl and beat together until well combined. (The mixture should be light and fluffy.)

3 Stir in the flour and millet flakes, the almonds and dried fruit. Put tablespoonfuls of the mixture on to the prepared baking sheets.

4 Bake for about 15 minutes until brown. Leave on the baking sheets for a few minutes, then transfer to a wire rack to cool completely.

Cornflake Caramel Slice

A wickedly decadent caramel layer nestles between the gluten-free base and the crispy cornflake topping. These cookies are simply irresistible – and fun to make too.

Makes 12

175g/6oz/¾ cup butter
150g/5oz/¾ cup caster (superfine) sugar
300g/10oz/2½ cups gluten-free flour
1 egg, beaten

For the topping

30ml/2 tbsp golden (light
  corn) syrup
397g/14oz can sweetened
  condensed milk
50g/2oz/¼ cup butter
90ml/6 tbsp sour cream
about 40g/1½oz/2 cups cornflakes
icing (confectioners') sugar (optional)

1 Preheat the oven to 190°C/375°F/ Gas 5. And proceed to line a 28 × 18cm/11 × 7in shallow cake tin (pan) with baking parchment.

2 Melt the butter in a pan, then remove from the heat. Put the sugar and flour in a bowl. Add the beaten egg and melted butter and mix well. Press the mixture evenly into the base of the prepared tin.

3 Bake for about 20 minutes until golden brown. Leave the base to cool completely in the tin.

4 For the topping, heat the syrup, condensed milk and butter over a low heat for 10–15 minutes, stirring occasionally, until the mixture is thick and turns a caramel colour.

5 Remove from the heat and stir in the sour cream. Spread over the base. Sprinkle over the cornflakes and leave to set. Sprinkle with icing sugar, if using, and cut into bars.

Double Chocolate Slices

These delicious gluten-free cookies have a smooth chocolate base, topped with a mint-flavoured cream and drizzles of melted chocolate. Perfect for a teatime treat – or at any time of day.

Makes 12

200g/7oz/1¾ cups gluten-free flour
25g/1oz/2 tbsp (unsweetened)
  cocoa powder
150g/5oz/⅔ cup unsalted (sweet) butter,
  cut into small pieces
75g/3oz/¾ cup icing
  (confectioners') sugar

For the topping

75g/3oz white chocolate mint crisps
50g/2oz/¼ cup unsalted (sweet)
  butter, softened
90g/3½oz/scant 1 cup icing
  (confectioners') sugar
50g/2oz milk chocolate

1 Preheat the oven to 180°C/350°F/Gas 4. Grease an 18cm/7in square shallow baking tin (pan) and line with a strip of baking parchment that comes up over two opposite sides. This will make it easier to remove the cookie base from the tin after baking.

2 Put the flour and cocoa powder into a food processor and add the pieces of butter. Process briefly until the mixture resembles fine breadcrumbs. Add the icing sugar and mix briefly again to form a smooth soft dough.

3 Turn the flour mixture into the prepared tin and gently press out to the edges with your fingers to make an even layer. Bake for 25 minutes, then remove from the oven and leave the base to cool completely in the tin.

4 To make topping, put the chocolate mint crisps in a polythene bag and tap firmly with a rolling pin until they are crushed. Beat the butter and sugar together until creamy, then beat in the crushed chocolate mint crisps. Spread the mixture evenly over the cookie base.

5 Melt the milk chocolate in a small heatproof bowl set over a pan of hot water. Lift the cookie base out of the tin; remove the paper. Using a teaspoon, drizzle the melted chocolate over the topping. Leave to set, then cut into squares.

Savoury Crackers

Cheese and biscuits is a classic after-dinner combination, but there are many other occasions when a savoury crunch is just what is needed. Crackers go well with home-made soup and salads for a light lunch and make delicious snacks when you want something with a little bite to it. This superb collection of tasty recipes offers something for all occasions, from sophisticated Wheat Thins to exotic Curry Crackers.

Wheat Thins

These classic wheat biscuits are especially delicious with rich-tasting creamy cheeses, and also make a quick snack simply spread with butter when you are in a hurry.

Makes 18

175g/6oz/1½ cups fine stoneground
    wholemeal (whole-wheat) flour
pinch of salt
5ml/1 tsp baking powder
50g/2oz/½ cup coarse oatmeal
40g/1½oz/3 tbsp granulated sugar
115g/4oz/½ cup unsalted (sweet) butter,
    chilled and diced

Cook's Tip

These cookies are perfect for serving with a cheeseboard and look very pretty cut into different shapes. You could make star-shaped cookies for Christmas, or heart-shaped ones for Valentine's Day.

1 Preheat the oven to 190°C/375°F/ Gas 5. Put all the ingredients into a food processor and process until the mixture starts to clump. Tip out on to a floured surface, gather the dough together with your hands and roll out.

2 Stamp out 18 rounds with a 7.5cm/3in round biscuit (cookie) cutter. Place on an ungreased baking sheet. Bake for 12 minutes until just beginning to colour at the edges. Leave to cool slightly, then transfer to a wire rack to cool completely.

Poppy Seed and Sea Salt Crackers

These attractive little crackers are ideal to use as the base of drinks party canapés, or they can be served plain as tasty nibbles in their own right.

Makes 20

115g/4oz/1 cup plain (all-purpose) flour
1.5ml/¼ tsp salt
5ml/1 tsp caster (superfine) sugar
15g/½oz/1 tbsp butter
15ml/1 tbsp poppy seeds
about 90ml/6 tbsp single (light) cream

For the topping

a little milk
sea salt flakes

Variation

You can use black or white poppy seeds – or a mixture of the two – for these crackers, or substitute sesame, caraway or celery seeds, if you like.

1 Preheat the oven to 150°C/ 300°F/Gas 2. Put the flour, salt and sugar in a bowl and rub in the butter. Stir in the poppy seeds. Add enough cream to mix to a stiff dough. Roll out on a lightly floured surface to a 20 x 25cm/8 x 10in rectangle. Cut into 20 squares.

2 Place the dough squares on an ungreased baking sheet and brush sparingly with milk. Sprinkle a few sea salt flakes over each cracker.

3 Bake in the oven for 30 minutes until crisp but still pale. Transfer to a wire rack to cool.

Polenta Chip Dippers

These tasty Parmesan-flavoured batons are best served warm from the oven with a spicy, tangy dip. A bowl of Thai chilli dipping sauce or a creamy, chilli-spiked guacamole are perfect.

2 Remove the pan from the heat and add the cheese, butter, pepper and salt to taste. Stir well until the butter has completely melted and the mixture is smooth.

3 Pour on to a smooth surface, such as a marble slab or a baking sheet. Spread the polenta out using a palette knife (metal spatula) to a thickness of 2cm/¾in and shape into a rectangle. Leave for at least 30 minutes to become quite cold. Meanwhile preheat the oven to 200°C/400°F/Gas 6 and lightly oil two or three baking sheets with some olive oil.

4 Cut the polenta slab in half, then carefully cut into even-size strips using a sharp knife.

5 Bake the polenta chips for about 40–50 minutes until they are dark golden brown and crunchy. Turn them over from time to time during cooking. Serve warm.

Cook's Tip

The unbaked dough can be made a day ahead, then wrapped in clear film (plastic wrap) and kept in the refrigerator until ready to bake.

Makes about 80

1.5 litres/2½ pints/6¼ cups water
10ml/2 tsp salt
375g/13oz/3¼ cups instant polenta
150g/5oz/1½ cups freshly grated
  Parmesan cheese
90g/3½oz/scant ½ cup butter
10ml/2 tsp cracked black pepper
olive oil, for brushing
salt

1 Put the water in a large heavy pan and bring to the boil over a high heat. Reduce the heat, add the salt and pour in the polenta in a steady stream, stirring constantly with a wooden spoon. Cook over a low heat, stirring constantly, until the mixture thickens and starts to come away from the sides of the pan – this will take about 5 minutes.

Herb and Garlic Twists

These twists are very short and crumbly, made with garlic-flavoured dough sandwiching with fresh herbs and some chilli flakes for an extra kick. A very popular party nibble.

Makes about 20

90g/3½oz/scant ½ cup butter, at room
    temperature, diced
2 large garlic cloves, crushed
1 egg
1 egg yolk
175g/6oz/1½ cups self-raising
    (self-rising) flour
large pinch of salt
30ml/2 tbsp chopped fresh mixed
    herbs, such as basil, thyme,
    marjoram and flat
    leaf parsley
2.5–5ml/½–1 tsp dried chilli flakes
paprika or cayenne pepper,
    for sprinkling

1 Preheat the oven to 200°C/400°F/ Gas 6. Put the butter and garlic into a bowl and beat well. Add the egg and yolk and beat in thoroughly. Stir in the flour and salt and mix to a soft but not sticky dough.

2 Roll the dough out on a sheet of baking parchment to a 28cm/11in square. Using a sharp knife, cut it in half to make two rectangles.

3 Sprinkle the herbs and chilli flakes over one of the rectangles, then place the other rectangle on top. Gently roll the rolling pin over the herbs and chilli flakes to press them into the dough.

4 Using a sharp knife, cut the dough into 1cm/½in sticks. Make two twists in the centre of each one and place on a non-stick baking sheet.

5 Bake the twists for 15 minutes, or until crisp and golden brown. Leave on the baking sheet to cool slightly, then carefully transfer to a wire rack to cool completely. To serve, sprinkle with a little paprika or cayenne pepper, according to taste.

Cook's Tip

If the dough seems a little too soft to handle, wrap it in clear film (plastic wrap) and chill in the refrigerator for about 15 minutes to firm up. It will be much easier to roll it out.

Parmesan Tuiles

These lacy tuiles look very impressive, but they couldn't be easier to make. Believe or not, they use only a single ingredient – Parmesan cheese.

Makes 8–10

115g/4oz Parmesan cheese

1 Preheat the oven to 200°C/400°F/ Gas 6. Line two baking sheets with baking parchment. Grate the cheese using a fine grater, pulling it down slowly to make long strands.

Cook's Tip
Tuiles can be made into little cup shapes by draping over an upturned egg cup. These little cups can be filled to make tasty treats to serve with drinks. Try a little cream cheese flavoured with herbs.

2 Spread the grated cheese out in 7.5–9cm/3–3½in rounds. Do not spread the cheese too thickly; it should just cover the parchment. Bake for 5–7 minutes until bubbling and golden brown.

3 Leave on the baking sheet for about 30 seconds and then carefully transfer, using a palette knife (metal spatula) to a wire rack. Alternatively, drape over a rolling pin to make a curved shape.

Three-cheese Crumble Cookies

A delicious combination of mozzarella, Red Leicester and Parmesan cheese and the fresh taste of pesto make these cookies totally irresistible. Make mini ones to serve with drinks.

Makes 10

225g/8oz/2 cups self-raising
    (self-rising) flour
50g/2oz/¼ cup butter, diced
50g/2oz mozzarella cheese, diced
50g/2oz Red Leicester cheese, diced
15ml/1 tbsp fresh pesto
1 egg
60ml/4 tbsp milk
15g/½oz/2 tbsp grated Parmesan cheese
15ml/1 tbsp mixed chopped nuts

1 Preheat the oven to 200°C/400°F/ Gas 6. Put the flour in a bowl and rub in the butter until the mixture resembles fine breadcrumbs.

2 Add the diced mozzarella and Red Leicester cheeses to the bowl and stir to mix well. In a separate bowl, beat together the pesto, egg and milk, then pour into the flour and cheese mixture. Stir together quickly until well combined.

3 Using a tablespoon, place in rocky piles on non-stick baking sheets. Sprinkle over the Parmesan cheese and chopped nuts. Bake for 12–15 minutes until well risen and golden brown. Transfer to a wire rack to cool.

Fennel and Chilli Ring Cookies

Based on an Italian recipe, these cookies are made with yeast and are dry and crumbly. Try them with drinks, dips or with antipasti.

Makes about 30

500g/1lb 2oz/4½ cups type 00 flour
115g/4oz/½ cup white vegetable fat
5ml/1 tsp easy-blend (rapid-rise) yeast
15ml/1 tbsp fennel seeds
10ml/2 tsp crushed chilli flakes
15ml/1 tbsp olive oil
400–550ml/14–18fl oz/1⅔–2½ cups
   lukewarm water
olive oil, for brushing

1 Put the flour in a bowl and rub in the fat until the mixture resembles fine breadcrumbs. Add the yeast, fennel and chilli and mix well. Add the oil and enough water to make a soft but not sticky dough. Turn out on to a floured surface and knead lightly.

2 Take small pieces of dough and shape into sausages about 15cm/6in long. Shape into rings and pinch the ends together.

3 Place the rings on a non-stick baking sheet and brush lightly with olive oil. Cover with a dishtowel and set aside at room temperature for 1 hour to rise slightly.

4 Meanwhile, preheat the oven to 150°C/300°F/Gas 2. Bake the cookies for 1 hour until they are dry and only slightly browned. Leave on the baking sheet to cool completely.

Cook's Tip

Type 00 is an Italian grade of flour used for pasta. It is milled from the centre part of the endosperm so that the resulting flour is much whiter than plain (all-purpose) flour. It contains 70 per cent of the wheat grain. It is available from Italian delicatessens and some large supermarkets. If you cannot find it, try using strong white bread flour instead.

Curry Crackers

Crisp curry-flavoured crackers are very good with creamy cheese or yogurt dips and make an unusual nibble with pre-dinner drinks. Add a pinch of cayenne pepper for an extra kick.

Makes about 30

175g/6oz/1½ cups self-raising
   (self-rising) flour
pinch of salt
10ml/2 tsp garam masala
75g/3oz/6 tbsp butter, diced
5ml/1 tsp finely chopped fresh
   coriander (cilantro)
1 egg, beaten

For the topping

beaten egg
black onion seeds
garam masala

1 Preheat the oven to 200°C/400°F/ Gas 6. Put the flour, salt and garam masala into a bowl. Rub in the butter until the mixture resembles fine breadcrumbs. Stir in the coriander, add the egg and mix to a soft dough.

Cook's Tip
Garam masala is a mixture of Indian spices, that usually contains a blend of cinnamon, cloves, peppercorns, cardamom seeds and cumin seeds. You can buy it ready-made or make your own.

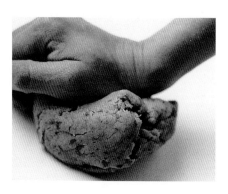

2 Turn out on to a lightly floured surface and knead gently until smooth. Roll out to a thickness of about 3mm/⅛in.

3 Using a fluted biscuit (cookie) wheel, knife or pizza wheel, cut the dough into neat rectangles measuring about 7.5 x 2.5cm/3 x 1in. Brush with a little beaten egg and sprinkle each cracker with a few black onion seeds. Place on non-stick baking sheets and bake in the oven for about 12 minutes until the crackers are light golden brown all over.

4 Remove from the oven and transfer to a wire rack using a palette knife (metal spatula). Put a little garam masala in a saucer and, using a dry pastry brush, dust each cracker with a little of the spice mixture. Leave to cool before serving.

index